More
Random
Acts
of
Kindness

More
Random
Acts
of
Kindness

The Editors of Conari Press

Conari Press
Berkeley, CA

Printed in the United States of America on recycled paper

Conari Press books are distributed by Publishers Group West

Cover: Sharon Smith Design; illustration: Cynthia Fitting; handlettering: Lily Lee; interior illustrations: Kathy Warinner

ISBN: 0-943233-82-8

Library of Congress Cataloging-in-Publication Data

More random acts of kindness / the editors of Conari Press.
p.   cm.
ISBN 0-943233-82-8 (trade paper) : $8.95
1. Kindness—Case studies. 2.Kindness—Quotations, maxims, etc.
I. Conari Press

BJ1533.K5M64   1994
177'.7—dc20   94-18839

10 9 8 7 6 5 4 3 2

So many gods, so many creeds,
So many paths that wind and wind,
While just the art of being kind
Is all the sad world needs.
—Ella Wheeler Wilcox

Profuse thanks to all those who shared their stories of random acts of kindness and in other ways contributed to the making of this book:

Judy Hart

Erika Hoving

Andy Bryner

Dawna Markova

Carla G. Reiber

Lori M. Kreis

Derrick Thomas

Varina D. Backest

Nila J. Webster

Mary Dempsey

Kriss Wagner

Paul & Pat Fenner

Anne C. Washburn

David Rogers

Priscilla Beard

Tad T. Miura

Caroline Reynolds

Karl J. Stone

Bernadette Debbs

Jerri A. Hutson

Al West

Victoria Cogswell

Ginger McDugle

Julie Perey

M. D'Ann Gayler

Elaine Sanders

Marion Edey

Angela Theresa Egic

Tina Martin	Pauline La Pierre
Sue Flynn	Joan Miller
Christy Conner	Jodi Bauer
Elizabeth A. Ely	Betty Litto
Barbara Gifford Dobbins	Sheri Olson
Marianne Schaedle	Patricia M. Fernberg
Linda M. Smith	Charlotte Parker
David Smith	Arianna Vander Houwen
Wendy Seadia	Kerry Patrick
Naomi McEneely	Dee Appel Tennant
Mara H. Wasburn	W.J. Lederer
Jeanne Winstead	Lisa M. Saris
Nancy Akerly	Michele M. Kemper
Jean A. McCollum	Dorothy M. Wagner
Claudia Schaab	Tessa McGlasson
June E. Andrew	Julie Bennett
Cindy Omusz	Kristin Braniff
Rita Grace Lash	Diana Apalategui
Amy Mulrooney	Frederick Peace
Jerry Curtis	Bonnie Burns

Tyann Sheldon

Ellen Levy

Susan H. Hirsch

Ralston Soong

Carol Baker

Karen Bouris

Jennifer Brontsema

Kathy Warinner

Emily Miles

Mary Jane Ryan

Will Glennon

Elizabeth von Radics

David Smith

Michele E. Miner

Michael Judd

David Wells

The Power
of
Random Acts of Kindness

$\mathcal{W}$e at Conari Press published *Random Acts of Kindness* to inspire and spread the word about the power of kindness. It did that and more: we have been flooded with letters from readers, telling us of the kindness they have experienced in their lives—simple acts that often left profound change in their wake. Each story was precious and powerful, from the simplest gesture to the most unimaginable miracle. *More Random Acts of Kindness* grew out of the realization that we could not possibly keep these stories to ourselves. Sifting through the piles of letters trying to pick which stories to publish was an almost impossibly difficult task. In the end we simply went on instinct, selecting those that moved us the most and offered the widest reflections on kindness.

Throughout the sorting process we noticed a few things about the inner workings of kindness as stories converged and themes repeated themselves over and over again. One of the obvious (and at first surprising) realizations was that most of the stories submitted, the ones people were almost desperate to tell, were invariably about kindnesses they had *received*. In each there was a giver and a receiver, but the need to tell the story was almost always from the person who had been the beneficiary.

At first we thought it was simply modesty. At a Random Acts of Kindness party we held, after many people had shared an act of kindness they had received, we pointed out that all the stories were from the point of view of the recipient and asked people to speak as well of the things they had done. The audience politely listened and then returned to telling the most fascinating and powerful stories of kindnesses done to and for them.

Gradually it became clear that the reason we were flooded with stories from recipients was really quite simple: the quality of the experience was dramatically different. The person on the receiving end experienced what was often a life-altering moment, whereas the giver experienced a less dramatic, quiet affirmation of simply having "done the right thing."

The second thing that emerged was that although the stories were as varied as the people telling them, at the foundation of each story was a very simple and compassionate connection between strangers who, for a moment, experienced one another not as strangers, but as family. In a sense, kindness truly *is* the acting out of our very deep and real connection to everyone and everything around us. It is the realization that all of us are in fact—not just in theory or theology—in this together.

The third observation is about the extraordinary impact of even the smallest act of kindness. Many of the experiences happened many years ago but made such an impression that they were every bit as powerful in the retelling. Just a simple story about a single act that occurred twenty years before could and frequently did call forth a deep well of emotion.

Most surprising was the realization of how easily we seem to misplace this jewel. Kindness is something we are accustomed to thinking of as "nice" or "sweet" and we tend to set it apart from those things we perceive of as more "important"—attributes like intelligence, strength, and power. It is so easy to see kindness as a wonderful quality in an individual but of limited importance in the complex life of work, achievement, politics, and society.

That framework arises almost naturally from the structure of our daily lives. We struggle with the immediate responsibilities of paying bills, raising children, and searching for answers to the personal, social, and global problems we face every day. And although kindness is a positive and valued attribute to carry with us in these endeavors, it doesn't always seem to play a role in the end results. It can look like an "extra something" that good people weave into their daily lives—but not a necessity.

From the vantage point of having read so many people's stories, however, we've come to see that this attitude misses the point entirely. Kindness is not about paying bills and getting by; its sphere of influence is vastly broader and ultimately more important. Kindness is about being who we truly are. Seen from this perspective, kindness emerges as one of the most powerful tools at our disposal as we go through our lives. Its power not only is easily accessible to anyone who cares to use it, but it also can never be diminished; rather it expands with every action. It has the ability to utterly transform another person's life through the simplest of actions. It has the capacity to return us to the very core of our humanity.

Even with this limitless power in our grasp, the texture and context of our lives often leave us confused about how to employ it. The desire is there—to connect, to lend a helping hand, to extend ourselves out into the world—but the avenues for doing so seem obscure and confused. We are often victims of our own fears and rationalizations—that the world is too dangerous a place to connect with, that one person cannot make a difference. Too many of us suffer from social shrinkage, reducing the boundaries within which we are willing to act from our hearts to smaller and smaller circles of friends and family.

When a mass tragedy occurs, people respond; floods in the Midwest, hurricanes in Florida, earthquakes in California, famine in Africa—all are met with an outpouring of kindness and generosity. Similarly, in most of the stories we received, the response had been triggered through the catalyst of someone else's unavoidable need. And while this is good, think of the untapped potential that would be unleashed if we could find a way to weave the kindness in our hearts into every moment of our lives.

That is the challenge: to learn how to practice random acts of kindness as a welcome and natural part of our daily lives. We see this book as a furthering of that learning.

—The Editors of Conari Press

A number of years back, my six-year-old son and I had gone shopping at one of those giant discount toy stores with toys piled to the ceiling. We had just come around the corner of an aisle when I saw a young, long-haired bearded man in a wheelchair. He must have been in some terrible accident because both his legs were missing and his face was badly scarred. Just then my six-year-old saw him too and said in a loud voice, "Look at that man, Momma!"

I did the normal mother thing and tried to shush my son, telling him it was not polite to point; but my son gave a hard tug, broke free from my hand, and went running down the aisle to the man in the wheelchair. He stood right in front of him and said in a loud voice, "What a cool dude earring, man! Where did you get such a neat earring?"

The young man broke into a grin that lit up his face. He was so taken aback by the compliment that he just glowed with happiness, and the two of them stood there talking awhile about his earring and other "cool stuff." It made a life-long impression on me. For I had seen only a horribly scarred man in a wheelchair, but my six-year-old saw a man with a cool dude earring.

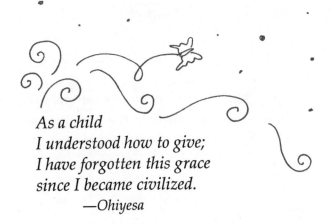

As a child
I understood how to give;
I have forgotten this grace
since I became civilized.
    —Ohiyesa

*Y*ears ago I had to have a new water heater installed. A very surly man showed up to do the installation, giving short, curt answers to my every question. I thought he was simply a sour old man and left him to his work.

When he finished, he said he had to wait for another worker to arrive to help him carry the old tank out of my basement. I invited him to sit in my kitchen and offered him some coffee. He said "Nope" and just sat down at my table with legs and arms crossed. I rolled my eyes and went about my work, knowing he'd be gone soon.

After a few moments he asked what was flashing on my dining room table. I retrieved a small clock shaped like a computer workstation and gave it to him to look at. I explained how it used solar power to alternately flash the time and the name of my company. He said "Hmmph" and set it on the kitchen table, but I noticed he continued to look at it from time to time.

Finally his assistant came and they carried the tank from the basement. He returned to my back door to get my signature, and I asked him to wait. I went in and got the clock and said, "Here, take this with you." He said, "Are you serious?" I said yes and smiled as he nodded and started to leave. He hesitated, turned back to me, and said, "Ya know, my wife died six weeks ago, and this is the first nice thing anyone's done for me." He looked at me one last moment, the corners of his mouth barely turning up, and walked away.

I walked back into my kitchen and broke down crying.

To give without any reward,
or any notice, has a special quality of its own.
—Anne Morrow Lindbergh

I am from a family of staunch Catholics, so my divorce was viewed as a disgrace and a scandal. My mother and I were estranged for over a year because of it. We started our reconciliation with tentative phone calls, letters, and my promise to come home for Christmas. Then she died unexpectedly on the first day of December. The plane tickets I had planned to use for a holiday reunion were instead used for her funeral. The black sheep returned to the fold.

For reasons of my own, I did not want to view the body in the casket. Many family members and friends questioned that decision,

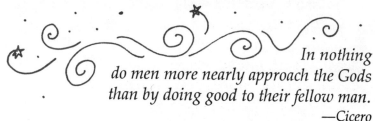

In nothing
do men more nearly approach the Gods
than by doing good to their fellow man.
—Cicero

but I sat resolutely in the reception parlor as the others went inside for prayers. In the middle of the throng, my most "perfect and pious" aunt—the mother of the priest—quietly announced, "I think I'll stay here too." She sat silently beside me and held my hand for the entire evening. The act was simple, the meaning immense. It happened thirteen years ago and I still cry when I remember how touched I was by her kindness.

Each person has inside a basic decency and goodness. If he listens to it and acts on it, he is giving a great deal of what it is the world needs most. It is not complicated but it takes courage. It takes courage for a person to listen to his own goodness and act on it.
        —*Pablo Casals*

$\mathcal{A}$ friend who was working in the Dominican Republic with Habitat for Humanity had befriended a small boy named Etin. He noticed that when Etin wore a shirt at all it was always the same dirty, tattered one. A box of used clothes had been left at the camp, and my friend found two shirts in it that were in reasonably good shape and about Etin's size, so he gave them to the grateful boy. A few days later he saw another boy wearing one of the shirts. When he next met up with Etin he explained that the shirts were meant for him. Etin just looked at him and said, "But you gave me two!"

What really matters is what you do with what you have.
—*Shirley Lord*

I had just moved to the San Francisco Bay Area and was worried about what seemed to be the increasing frequency of carjackings. Whenever I drove I was constantly aware of my surroundings and was always taking steps to avoid becoming a "statistic." One morning I was in a particularly bad area, sitting at an intersection waiting for the light to change. As I looked across the street, I saw several men grouped around a stopped car. One man was moving in and out of the driver's side with such intensity and effort that he looked as though he was using all his strength.

My heart jumped into my throat as I thought I was witnessing someone being carjacked. But before my brain could come up with any action to take, I realized that the man's car had stalled, and with the help of the other men he was trying to push it to the side of the street. As I watched, they pushed it to safety and after a wave and a nod they all walked off in different directions. Total strangers helping someone out. I felt like crying—whether at the unexpected sweetness of the scene or at my unwarranted suspicion and fright—I do not know.

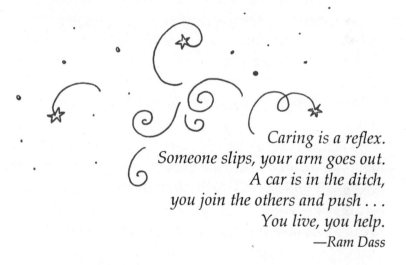

Caring is a reflex.
Someone slips, your arm goes out.
A car is in the ditch,
you join the others and push . . .
You live, you help.
—Ram Dass

There is a beautiful old spruce tree that grows in a field alongside the street to my home. For years it has been a comforting and serene part of my daily commute. Over the past few years I had watched a thick vine grow around the tree and climb its trunk. As time went by the vine grew more and more vigorously, and the poor old tree was clearly suffering. I don't know why I simply observed and did nothing.

One Saturday morning as I was driving my children into town for assorted sporting events, I noticed a elderly couple had driven into the field and were rummaging around in their car. Returning home many hours later I saw the couple sweating away in the hot sun, doing mortal battle with the massive vine. I quickly changed into my yard clothes, mixed up a pitcher of lemonade, threw an assortment of fruit and snacks into a cooler, and headed over to the field.

When I got there I was astounded by what I saw: the couple had been hacking away for half the day already, and a huge pile of cut vines with stems as thick as a garden hose lay next to the tree. But there was much more to be done. I greeted the couple with my offerings and after a brief, friendly picnic we all set to the task at hand.

By the end of the day we had attracted three more volunteers, and by sunset you could almost hear the sigh of relief from that old spruce. Our efforts were not in vain; now whenever I drive past my heart fills with joy over the robust appearance of that beautiful tree.

My satisfaction comes from my commitment to advancing a better world.
—Faye Wattleton

*D*riving the fourteen miles home to our small Iowa town from a last-minute Christmas shopping trip, my father was carefully navigating his way through the heavy falling snow. About a half-mile from our farmhouse—the only one for miles—we spotted a car in the ditch and stopped to investigate. It was empty. The blowing snow all but obscured the lane up to our house, but I could see that the lights were on and we *never* left the lights on.

As we stumbled in our front door we were greeted by the refugees from the abandoned car, a stranded family of four. They began apologizing for being in our house, but Mom just said, "Shush, you did what you had to do," as she began preparing hot drinks and food for us all.

It seemed so natural to expect them to stay the night, so my brother and I eagerly began getting acquainted with our new friends. Farm life was lonely for the two of us, age eight and ten, and the company of other boys was always welcome. That night the full force of the storm hit and by morning it was obvious that our guests would not be able to continue their journey to Minnesota for Christmas. There was two feet of snow everywhere and probably no snowplow for days. To four small boys it was paradise.

Mom just took us aside and we began to rewrap and address presents for our newly-found extended family. Unbeknownst to us, the father had gone back to their car to collect their Minnesota presents and was doing the same. It was one of the best Christmases I can remember.

After the verb "to love," the verb, "to help" is the most beautiful verb in the world.
—*Bertha Von Suttner*

21

I arrived at the airport in Pullman, Washington, excited about my approaching interview for admission to the University of Washington's veterinary school. I went directly to the rental-car agency to pick up my car, only to find, to my disbelief and horror, that my credit card had been refused and I had no other means of payment.

I ran to the pay phone and called my roommate back in California. I was trying to explain what had happened in between hysterical sobs, when a man walked up to me, tapped me on the shoulder, handed me a hundred-dollar bill, and walked away. Thanks to the generous compassion of a total stranger I made the interview on time and was accepted into the veterinary school.

Only a life lived for others is worth living.
—*Albert Einstein*

When we were in our early twenties my best friend and I spent six months traveling throughout Europe. We had bought train tickets in Italy to go to Greece via Yugoslavia. Once on board the government-run train, a pair of Yugoslav soldiers entered our compartment to collect our tickets. The blond one, who seemed to be the one in charge, immediately became abusive. Though they spoke no English, I managed to communicate through the dark-haired soldier, who spoke broken French. Apparently our tickets were insufficient to get us to Greece, and the blond soldier demanded money on the spot. Unsure whether our tickets really were inadequate or if

It's the small things that are hard to do.
—*John B. Flannagan*

this was simply an extortion attempt, we swore we had no money on us. The blond soldier then proceeded to confiscate our passports and lock us in our compartment, where we stayed for two days and nights with only a little water and some chocolate.

Soldiers barged into our compartment around the clock, often with dogs, always with guns, each time asking for our identification, as if they didn't already know who we were. The blond was usually among them and he was always gruff and intimidating, often leering at my friend. We saw the dark-haired interpreter a few times, but he rarely spoke. Eventually the blond soldier said we would not be able to leave

Just do what must be done.
This may not be happiness, but it is greatness.
—*George Bernard Shaw*

the country and that we would be turned over to the Yugoslav police.

As we approached the border, pondering our predicament and wondering if we should reveal to them our $500 in travelers' checks, the dark-haired soldier suddenly slipped into our compartment and motioned us toward the back of the car. As our train came to a halt at the checkpoint, he pointed to a local train on the next track. As we jumped to the ground, he quickly handed us our passports, three apples, and two tickets to the first Greek town over the border. Then he was gone.

When you are kind to someone in trouble,
you hope they'll remember
and be kind to someone else.
And it'll become like a wildfire.
—*Whoopi Goldberg*

*T*he year I went away to college was a very difficult transition for me. I lived in Oregon and had hauled my earthly possessions all the way to Southern California to a place I had never been before and was surrounded by people I didn't know. As is probably true with many people, I got quite homesick and many times contemplated going home.

Although the highlight of the day for many students is getting letters from home, my mailbox was frequently empty, which did nothing to ease my unhappiness. One day when I went to the mailbox, there was a postcard staring out at me. I sat down to read it, expecting a note from someone back home. But I became increasingly confused as I understood none of the postcard: It was a full news report about a woman named Mabel and the recent birth of her very ugly baby. I double-checked the address and, yes, it was addressed to me—with no return address. Still confused, I took the card back to my dorm room and forgot about it.

Several days later I received another postcard, this one delivering news about Maybelline, Mabel's copycat cousin who had also had a baby, and their matching FBI husbands. Soon after another card arrived and then another. Each card grew progressively more bizarre, full of news of people riding horses into Safeway, remembrances of my birthday on the yacht in Madrid, and so on. I began to really look forward to the next installment, interested to see what this mystery writer would come up with next. I

Let a good person do good deeds
with the same zeal that an evil person does bad ones.
—*Shalom Rokeach*

was never disappointed.

Eventually, the cards stopped coming, right about the time I had begun to feel a part of college life. They had been such an entertaining distraction that I hardly noticed the change at first.

When I went home on a break I visited an old high-school friend and told her about my mystery correspondent. She hesitated a moment, then told me that her mother had wanted to make sure I got some mail while I was at school but didn't have a lot to say, so she just made up things.

I have saved all her postcards and still bring them out to read now and then whenever I need a lift.

Life's most persistent and urgent question is, What are you doing for others?
        —*Martin Luther King, Jr.*

*M*y marriage had come apart in a dramatic and violent fashion that left me shaking and scared to death. I escaped with two small children, a broken-down car, and $423 in cash. I was so scared that I drove aimlessly for hundreds of miles, determined to get so completely lost that I could not be found. Not a single person knew where we had gone. After sleeping in the car for a couple of days, I found a run-down old house outside a small town and put down almost the last of my money for rent. I was scared and broke but at least we had a place to start over. I spent the next day looking for work and came "home" to our sad and empty nest on the verge of tears, not at all sure we would make it.

There, sitting on the sagging front porch were five bags of groceries, a large box of pots, pans, and kitchen utensils, and a vase of the most beautiful irises I had ever seen. I must have cried for ten minutes before I could pull myself together to unpack our miraculous gifts. No note, no explanation. I could not imagine who could have done it, who could possibly have known how desperate we were. That was many years ago, and sitting on top of my stove in my beautiful modern kitchen is an old, battered whistle-blowing teapot, reminding me when I boil water for my morning coffee of the beautiful gift of kindness that was given to me in my hour of greatest need.

He who wishes to secure the good of others
has already secured his own.
　　—*Confucius*

I was always a very conscientious student and in my entire school career was late to class only once. I was seven years old and, of course, it had to happen when I was just starting a new school (my third that year). Even though it wasn't my fault, I was terribly embarrassed and afraid, particularly since I was very shy and did not know the other children. Tears were streaming down my face as I ran the final blocks to school. As I passed the house across from the school, a well-dressed man came to the gate. I had never met him, but I knew his name because he was one of my town's most prominent citizens. He said to me, "Little girl, what is the trouble?" I blurted out my story, and he pulled out an immaculate white handkerchief, wiped away my tears, and told me that the dour Mrs. Morris—the school principal—was a friend of his and that he would go with me to help me sort out the difficulties.

He took my hand and walked me to school. In the principal's office he made excuses for me and asked that as a special favor I be let off without a reprimand. When he finished talking, I could see that "dour" Mrs. Morris was having trouble not laughing. I was never again afraid of her. She walked me to my class and told the teacher that new children were allowed one unrecorded "tardy." I was an instant celebrity—a shy stranger no longer.

Sympathy: Two hearts tugging at one load.
—*Charles H. Parkhurst*

An adventurous group of Australians had arrived in Nepal in an attempt to climb Mt. Everest. At the ten-thousand-foot level, one of the group became very sick with chills, fever, nausea, and vomiting. His "friends" wrapped him up in his sleeping bag and continued their climb. Two weeks later, he woke up in a Sherpa village. They had found him on the mountainside, where he had slipped into a coma, and had brought him to their village to nurse him back to health.

It took many months for him to fully regain his health. Finally, six months after being abandoned on the mountainside he returned to the

With every deed you are sowing a seed, though the harvest you may not see.
—*Ella Wheeler Wilcox*

Australian embassy in Katmandu to find that his passport had been turned in by his climbing partners with the explanation that he had died on the slopes of Mt. Everest.

The man who had been so lovingly nursed back to health was—in his life in Australia—a trained nurse. After having his worldly possessions sent to him from home, he returned to the Sherpas to repay their kindness by living, working, and caring for his new "chosen people."

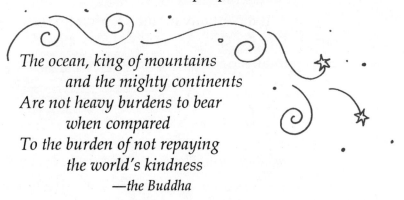

The ocean, king of mountains
*   and the mighty continents*
Are not heavy burdens to bear
*   when compared*
To the burden of not repaying
*   the world's kindness*
*   —the Buddha*

*M*y sister lives in a small town in Germany. She wanted to have a nightstand lamp repaired, so she wrapped it up and put it in a shopping bag and boarded the bus to the nearest large town. When she arrived at the repair shop she realized sheepishly that she had left her bag on the bus. She called the bus company and asked if they would return the shopping bag to her the next day if it was found.

The next morning she went down to the bus station at the appointed time and they handed her the bag with the lamp in it, only now the

*Whatever we do for someone else
we do because it fulfills a need we have.*
—M. Scott Peck

35

lamp worked perfectly! She called the bus company and discovered that the bus driver—a man obviously very handy with such things—had discovered the bag, seen that the lamp was broken, and between routes had repaired it. The next day the bus driver was delivered a still-steaming loaf of my sister's fantastic home-made bread.

Past the seeker as he prayed, came the crippled
and the beggar and the beaten. And seeing them,
the holy one went down into deep prayer and cried,
"Great God, how is it that a loving creator can see such
things and yet do nothing about them?"
And out of the long silence, God said,
"I did do something. I made you."
—Sufi teaching story

*M*y son is wheelchair-bound from a head injury he suffered in an accident last year. He recently decided he wanted a kitten to keep him company and started watching the classified ads in the local paper. An ad finally appeared, and after calling to make sure there were still kittens available, I drove across town to pick one up for him. When I got there I found the last kitten cuddled up in the arms of a young man named Ron.

*At some point
your heart will tell itself what to do.*
—*Achaan Chah*

I was disappointed because I knew how excited my son was and it must have shown on my face. I told the young man my story, and he graciously smiled, handed me the kitten, and told me not to worry—he would find another one. As I sit and watch the joy on my son's face when he plays with that little black-and-white cat, I can't help but think of that wonderfully generous young man.

In the long run, we get no more than we have been willing to risk giving.
—*Sheldon Kopp*

*T*he approach of my daughter's high school graduation had been emotionally unsettling; I was so proud and happy for her and yet was already feeling the sadness of her eventually leaving the nest. On the morning of her graduation I received a telephone call informing me of the death from lung cancer of one of my oldest and dearest friends. I was devastated by the news and thrown into a state of emotional overload. I felt like I could neither properly grieve my friend's death nor celebrate my daughter's graduation.

At the ceremony with "Pomp

When a blind man carries a lame man, both go forward.
—*Swedish proverb*

and Circumstances" playing in the background, another dear friend appeared, carrying an armload of long-stemmed yellow roses. She plucked one out and handed it to me with a hug and a kiss and moved on to find other mothers with graduating children.

I watched her go, overflowing with the love she had imparted, and remembered that only a few years earlier she had lost her husband, the love of her life for more than twenty years, to the same deadly disease that had taken my friend that day.

When it comes to getting things done,
we need fewer architects and more bricklayers.
—Colleen C. Barrett

My husband and beloved friend died very suddenly last October. Knowing how difficult the first Christmas without him would be, I decided to take my teenaged daughters to New Orleans for the holidays, hoping that different surroundings would make it a little easier. I was mistaken—nothing could ease the pain.

We decided to make the eight-hour drive home on cold and dreary Christmas day. You would think that the radio would be filled with Christmas songs, but instead every song sang out words of love and loss. The clouds and grayness of dusk mirrored my grief, and after a while I could no longer stand the confinement of the car and asked my daughter to pull over and let me out.

I walked beside the highway in the damp weeds, sobbing in pain while my daughters followed slowly on the shoulder of the road. Suddenly out of the enclosing darkness came the voice of a woman, asking me if I was all right. She came to me and held me in her arms, and, with my daughters following, took me in her car to her home where she served us tea. Before seeing us on our way with renewed spirits, she led us to a nearby town famous for its beautiful Christmas lights. She was truly a Christmas angel.

The best and most beautiful things in the world cannot be seen or even touched. They must be felt with the heart.
—Helen Keller

*W*hen I was working in Washington, D.C., I used to take the Metro to work. Every morning as I got off the subway and rode the escalator up to street level I would hear the same man's voice booming in the manner of Robin Williams in the movie *Good Morning Vietnam*, only his message was "GOOD MORNING AMERICA!" I was not amused. I was always in a hurry, he was half blocking the exit off the escalator, and sometimes he would look at me and speak directly to me. I for one just wished he would go away.

One morning during the Christmas season as I stepped onto the escalator I could hear this beautiful, lyrical, a cappella version of "Joy to the World" greeting me. The familiar song was being sung in a clear tenor, and the words and music were so bright and beautiful that I felt like I was hearing the carol for the first time. My heart skipped a beat and tears came to my eyes as I rode up the escalator bathed in the blessing of this perfect song.

Sure enough, it was Mr. Good Morning America, standing off to the side, today with his eyes closed, giving us all a wonderful Christmas present as we stepped onto the pavement to face our workday. I have carried that stranger's precious gift with me ever since and I often silently thank him for giving me a memory I will always cherish.

Too many people are ready to carry the stool when the piano needs to be moved.
—Anonymous

*M*y brother is a teacher who doubles as the golf coach for an inner-city high school. When his first "team" showed up, he had four excited boys—only one of whom had even played miniature golf—and no equipment. Doing what he could, he scrounged up some old clubs from his and our father's collection and managed to put together three mismatched sets that they could share.

One day he was playing golf with some people he didn't know, and mentioned in the course of the conversation his golf team and their unusual equipment. The next Monday morning he was called down to the school office. One of the men he had played golf with had shown up at the school with four complete sets of clubs, with golf bags and wood covers, each equipped with three dozen new balls.

My brother wanted to thank the man but didn't remember his name, so he wrote a letter to the local newspaper and it ran on the front page of the sports section. Within two weeks the school had received so much equipment they were able to donate several sets of clubs to other inner-city schools for their fledgling golf teams.

Die when I may,
I want it said of me by those who knew me best,
that I always plucked a thistle
and planted a flower where I thought a flower would grow.
    —Abraham Lincoln

*T*welve years ago I came home from grocery shopping to a message that my husband had been killed in a freak auto accident. Totally aside from the devastating emotional toll it took on me, I was completely unprepared to cope with the myriad things that needed to be done. Without asking, or for that matter seemingly without any planning whatsoever, my neighbors simply extended their circle of chores to encompass my small farm.

One day my cornfield was harvested; repairs to my roof and barn just appeared. My vegetable garden seemed always weeded and more productive than ever before—soon vegetables that I didn't remember having planted were ripening. I would come home to find a pile of wood, cut and stacked and ready to get me through the winter. Pies, breads, and jams, and cases of canned tomatoes appeared at my door and in my pantry.

It all seems so unreal now: whatever was needed simply manifested. When it was no longer needed, it no longer appeared. It was like some kind of beautiful self-correcting dance of kindness. I will be forever grateful to all those wonderful people.

Kindness is an inner desire
that makes us want to do good things
even if we do not get anything in return.
It is the joy of our life to do them.
When we do good things from this inner desire, there is
kindness in everything we think, say, want, and do.
　　　　—*Emanuel Swedenborg*

When I was about twelve I used to visit this elderly gentleman who was a volunteer merit-badge counselor for the Boy Scouts. He would meet with scouts over a period of time and give them assignments until he deemed them proficient in their understanding of the particular subject. Although I did not know him long, I

Most people really believe that the Christian commandments (e.g., to love one's neighbor as oneself) are intentionally a little too severe—like putting the clock ahead half an hour to make sure of not being late in the morning.
—*Soren Kierkegaard*

admired him because of his service to our community, even while he was in poor health.

One day I was scheduled to meet with him to go over an assignment he had given me, but I forgot about it until some three hours later. I hopped on my bike and pedaled furiously to his home, all the while fretting about how poorly he must think of me for being an irresponsible Boy Scout. When I got to his house his wife answered the door and I blurted out my apology, but I could tell that something was wrong. She paused and then told me that her husband had just died. Then she apologized for not having had time to inform our scoutmaster. I left her home wondering if some-

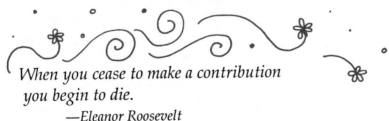

When you cease to make a contribution
you begin to die.
—*Eleanor Roosevelt*

how my failure to keep the appointment had disappointed him so much that he died.

Some thirty years later I told this story to a friend. I said that though I had long since realized that my lateness had nothing to do with his death, I could not help but wonder if I could have made a difference had I shown up on time. My friend quickly commented that my not being there was probably meant to be, since the situation would have been too traumatic for me. Hearing her say that was like a huge wave hitting me and lifting off this heavy weight I'd been carrying for years. Now whenever I think of that kind old gentleman, I think too of the kind words of my friend.

A person who seeks help for a friend,
while needy himself, will be answered first.
—*the Talmud*

I am sixteen years old and still learning about who I am and how to live. One weekend I went with a boyfriend to his family reunion. I felt very uncomfortable and didn't know what to say. I ended up sitting next to his grandfather. He started to tell me all about his late wife, their first date, engagement, and marriage, and their last days together. He spoke with such genuine feeling that for two hours I laughed and cried and was completely captured by his incredible stories. By the time I had to go it felt like I was sitting next to a close friend, and I was reluctant to leave this man who had entrusted me with such precious memories and had made me feel so included. I broke up with my boyfriend shortly afterward, but I will never forget that conversation.

What one does is what counts
and not what one had the intention of doing.
—*Pablo Picasso*

*F*or several years I suffered with a failing heart. Last summer as its strength waned dangerously toward complete failure, I was finally put on a list of patients waiting for heart transplants. By then my health was so precarious I was unable to do even the simplest act of shopping or cooking. The daily walk to the mailbox left me winded and weak. If I were to list all the acts of kindness that were shown to me during that time it would fill a full page of a newspaper. But one act stands out—that of the parents who lost their teenager in a horrible accident. In the midst of their anguish and indescribable grief, they gave me the gift of life: their child's heart. From the very depths of that heart—my heart—flow gratitude, sympathy, and prayers.

Live as if everything you do will eventually be known.
—*Hugh Prather*

When most people think of the telephone company, *kindness* is not a word that comes to mind. But telephone companies are staffed by people, and where people gather, kindness is never too far away. A service representative for a midwestern phone company had taken a call from an elderly woman wanting to make payment arrangements. She learned during the course of the call that the woman was housebound due to bad weather, was out of heart medication, and, because of her tight budget, was eating only one meal a day.

Service is the rent we pay for being.
It is the very purpose of life and not something
you do in your spare time.
—*Marian Wright Edelman*

Many phone calls later to different volunteer agencies in the area, the operator had arranged for the woman to receive medication and a weekly visit by a nurse, regular deliveries of food, and assistance with her utility bills. All of this was accomplished without fanfare and without ever telling the woman who had done the legwork.

If you want happiness for an hour—take a nap.
If you want happiness for a day—go fishing.
If you want happiness for a month—get married.
If you want happiness for a year—inherit a fortune.
If you want happiness for a lifetime—help someone else.
—Chinese proverb

While riding the bus to work one day, I noticed a small boy—no more than six or seven—board the bus. I was surprised that no adult accompanied him. With an oversized backpack on his back, it was obvious he was on his way to school, and he asked the driver to call out his stop. He sat so adultlike in the front of the bus. I watched as his small legs dangled off the seat, unable to reach the floor. The bus driver called out

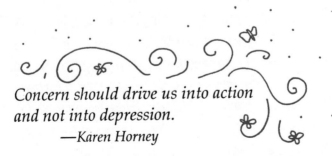

Concern should drive us into action and not into depression.
—*Karen Horney*

his stop and waited patiently while the boy attempted to cross the busy street. Cars continued to whiz by. Then the driver put on the emergency brake, stepped off the bus, and took the boy's hand to lead him across the street. My heart filled with emotion. As I was leaving I got the driver's name and wrote a letter to the transit company, thanking them for having such a wonderful employee.

Time is the one commodity above all that is our true possession. . . . Time's most important quality is that it passes, that we have only a finite amount. Therefore, be aware of its value and know that when you give your time, you're giving of your life.
—*Daphne Rose Kingma*

*I*t was the middle of winter and I had been driving around for weeks with a backseat full of old clothes to drop off at a local charity. For some reason, even though I drove past the collection point every day, I just kept forgetting to stop. One night after my shift had ended at midnight, I was driving home through downtown. The streets were deserted except for a man who was walking with just a blanket thrown over a thin cotton shirt to ward off the bitter cold.

The white man knows how to make everything, but he does not know how to distribute it.
—*Sitting Bull*

I pulled a coat, down vest, and some gloves out of the pile in the backseat and, after driving a roundabout course to get through all the one-way streets, finally caught up with him. Jumping out of the car with the clothes I ran up to him and said, "I hope they fit." I can still see the smile that spread across his face, and he thanked me. I hurried back to my warm car and I was smiling too and a lot more thankful for all that I have to spare.

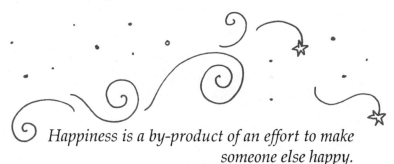

Happiness is a by-product of an effort to make someone else happy.
—*Gretta Brooker Palmer*

*M*any years ago my wife and I and our three children were in France for the Christmas holidays. The five days leading up to Christmas were an increasingly depressing series of minor disasters. On Christmas Eve we checked into a dingy hotel in Nice with no holiday cheer in our hearts.

It was raining and cold when we went out for dinner. We ended up in a drab little restaurant, too tired and miserable to search any further. Inside only five tables were occupied, two German couples, two French couples, and an American sailor sitting by himself. In the corner a piano player listlessly played Christmas music. Everyone sat eating in stony silence; only the sailor seemed happy, writing a letter as he ate.

My wife ordered our meal in French. The waiter brought the wrong thing. I scolded my wife for being stupid and she began to cry. On our right one of the German wives began berating her husband. On our left a French father slapped his son for some minor infraction and the boy began to cry.

We were all interrupted by an unpleasant blast of cold air as an old, thoroughly drenched French flower woman came in and made the rounds with her basket of flowers but had no takers. Wearily she sat down at a table and said to the waiter, "A bowl of soup. I haven't sold any flowers all afternoon." Then to the piano player she said, "Can you imagine, Joseph, soup on Christmas Eve?" He simply pointed to his empty tip jar.

The young sailor got up after finishing his meal, walked over to the flower woman, and, picking up two small corsages, said, "Happy Christmas, how much are these?" The women told him two francs. He handed her a twenty-franc note, kissed her cheek, and said, "The rest is my Christmas present to you." He quickly walked to our table, handed one of the corsages to my wife, and departed.

Everyone stopped eating and for a moment the restaurant was completely silent, then Christmas exploded like a bomb. The old flower woman jumped up doing a jig and, waving the twenty-franc note, shouted to the piano player, "Joseph, my Christmas present; and you shall have half so you can fete too."

The piano player began beating out "Good King Wenceslas," and my wife, waving her corsage in time to the music, began to sing. Our children joined in and the Germans jumped up on their chairs and began singing in German. The waiter embraced the flower woman, the French boy climbed onto his father's lap, and both joined in with the swelling international choir.

The Germans ordered wine for everyone, delivering it themselves accompanied by hugs and Christmas greetings. One of the French families followed suit with Champagne and kisses. The owner of the restaurant began singing "The First Noel," and everyone joined in—half of us with tears in our eyes—and people began crowding in from the street until the place was packed with diners while the Christmas songs rolled on.

Just minutes earlier eighteen people were spending a miserable evening in the same room. It ended up with all of us sharing one of the very best Christmas Eves we had ever experienced—all because one young sailor held the Christmas spirit in his soul.

*Without the human community
one single human being cannot survive.*
—the Dalai Lama

I was the new kid at my high school and, being very shy, I found it hard to make friends. My escape was volleyball. I love to play and was good enough to get on the girls' varsity team. Most of the girls on the team were pretty nice, but they had been playing together for three years and I was clearly the outsider. The third game of the season was our biggest challenge; we had to play the state champions and they had an absolutely awesome player on their team named Angela.

We knew we didn't have much chance but we at least wanted to play well. I think I played okay, but I don't remember doing anything that special. Anyway, we lost, but we forced the match to go three games and were even ahead for a little while. When we were collecting our stuff after the game, Angela walked up, pointed her finger right at me, and said, "You are good, girl!" Then she smiled and walked away.

I was so surprised I was almost embarrassed until my whole team came running over to hug me. On the way back to the bus, one of my teammates turned to me and said, "Next year we'll beat them, because Angela is graduating and we've still got you."

We realize that what we are accomplishing is a drop in the ocean. But if this drop were not in the ocean, it would be missed.
—Mother Teresa

*T*wenty-five years ago, I was riding in a taxicab in Amsterdam and saw a mother duck crossing the street ahead of us with a long line of ducklings waddling behind her. The cab driver never even attempted to slow down; he just plowed through them. It was a sickening moment, and even though it happened so long ago I can still feel the wrenching in my stomach every time I see ducks walking. The healing balm for that memory finally showed up today in a tiny story in my local newspaper:

"She kept an anxious vigil, pacing back and forth like a nervous basketball coach at a crucial game. If she had hands, she would have been wringing them nonstop. But she didn't. She was a duck. A duck with a lot at stake, no less. During a morning waddle across Fallen Leaf Circle in San Ramon Thursday, her five tiny ducklings had slipped between the two-inch slit in a storm-drain grate.

"Cars passed and people walked by, but neither man nor vehicle nor Animal Control could sway her from her post. At last, rescue arrived. Out of nowhere, four burly guys from Public Works and Animal Control Services—one or two who looked like they'd treat a duck about as gently as a bowling ball—unbolted the grate and stepped tenderly down the drain so they didn't scare the little fellas.

"One of them scooped up the ducklings and set them down in a white plastic bucket, cradling each one like a precious gem. They poured the ducklings into a nearby creek and the little family was last seen paddling off into the sunrise."

I am only one; but still I am one.
I cannot do everything, but still I can do something.
I will not refuse to do the something I can do.
—*Helen Keller*

*C*alifornia recently enacted what is euphemistically called the "three strikes you're out" law. It decrees that anyone convicted of a third felony is to be sentenced to a minimum prison term of twenty-five years to life. The campaign for this law had been characterized by the all-too-present fear of and anger about violent crime; but the law itself went much further, sentencing *any* third-time felon to a lifetime in prison regardless of the nature of the crime. One of the first cases to be prosecuted under the new law, however, quickly ran into an unanticipated problem—the victim.

The criminal, a forty-five-year-old repeat petty offender, was spotted breaking into a car and trying to walk away with an armful of clothes. The police did their job, and the local district attorney geared up to enforce the new law, until the victim—a seventy-year-old woman—refused to cooperate because she was appalled at its harshness: "I just think it's really gross; I couldn't enjoy another sunny day myself if he was never going to see one." Instead of life in prison, the burglar was sentenced to four years, plenty of time to contemplate the compassion of his victim.

To do good is to do so in the minute particular.
The general good is the refuge of the fool
and the scoundrel.
—*William Blake*

*W*hen I was six years old my mother took me to school on opening day. Sometime during that first day, a small boy started to cry. I immediately went over to him and put my arms around him. The teacher ordered me to return to my assigned seat. I could not believe this teacher's indifference toward this boy because whenever I cried at home, some member of my family would be right there with their arms around me.

My teacher kept telling me to leave the boy alone, and I kept refusing to obey her until the boy stopped crying. I went home that day with a note to my mother stating that I was rude, disobedient, and a troublemaker. I explained to my mother just what had happened, and she came back to school with me the next day. She told my teacher that I had been taught to be considerate and caring toward others and that I was not likely to change. She strongly advised my teacher to get used to my sympathetic nature.

That incident happened seventy-two years ago, and I have enjoyed hugging a lot of troubled people since then.

If I can stop one heart from breaking,
I shall not live in vain:
If I can ease one life the aching,
Or cool one pain,
Or help one fainting robin
Unto his nest again,
I shall not live in vain.
—Emily Dickinson

A few years ago I had managed to screw up my life so badly that I found myself without a home and without hope. I'm ashamed to admit it, but even then I was so absorbed by my own self-pity that all I could think of was begging enough money to buy the cheapest drink I could find. One day I was sitting in front of a store panhandling when a woman walked by with a small boy in tow. She ignored my pitch and hurried away. As I watched them go down the sidewalk the small boy broke free and came running back. He stood in front of me, fumbling in his coat pocket; he

We have to move beyond
the mind-set of powerlessness.
—*Audrey Edwards*

pulled out a five-dollar bill that was almost certainly more money than he had ever held before, and handed it to me.

I was completely dumbstruck and just sat there staring at him with the money in my hand. By then his mother had returned and with tears in her eyes gently led the boy away. He turned back once to wave and they were gone. I don't know how long I sat there, but I have not had another drink since then.

Noble deeds and hot baths
are the best cures for depression.
—Dodie Smith

I had a wonderful, funny, caring neighbor named Ed whom I lived next to for fifteen years. Ed developed a terminal cancer, and as he gradually weakened, his wife became the sole breadwinner. Knowing how difficult just the daily routine was, I began cooking dinner for them one night a week. Ed and I shared a love for Jell-O, and each week I would try out a new variation. Since my family did not really care for Jell-O, this was a special treat for me as well.

Every Wednesday night at 6 P.M. I'd bring over their dinner, and every Wednesday at 7 P.M. I'd receive a call from Ed, thanking me.

A person's true wealth is the good he or she does in the world.
—*Mohammed*

Sadly, this ritual lasted only a few months; Ed passed away at Thanksgiving.

I had put that time out of my mind until about a year later. I was making Jell-O, and all those times with Ed came flooding back. Shortly before he died Ed had written me a beautiful note, thanking me for what I had been doing. As I was mixing the Jell-O I wished I had thanked him for the weekly gift he gave me. Through those times with Ed I learned that it truly was better to give than to receive and that you cannot give kindness without spreading some of it on yourself.

Engrave this upon my heart: There isn't anyone you couldn't love once you've heard their story.
—Mary Lou Kownacki, OSB

*T*he fall semester of my senior year in college was a particularly stressful one. My mother had just died after a battle with cancer, and I knew it would be difficult to cope with this loss and also juggle a campus job and a full courseload. I never imagined I would be as unhappy as I was by the end of the semester. One day, after spending many hours studying for finals, I checked my mailbox and found two tickets for a John Cougar Mellencamp concert the next evening. There was a note

Injustice, poverty, slavery, ignorance—
these may be cured by reform or revolution.
But [people] do not live only by fighting evils.
They live by positive goals, individual and collective, a
vast variety of them, seldom predictable.
       —Sir Isaiah Berlin

attached that said, "Relax and enjoy yourself!" No name, no return address.

I was thrilled to be able to go to the concert but felt even better just knowing that someone had noticed how difficult the changes in my life had been. I asked all my friends, and everyone denied having sent me the tickets. I have no idea who was so kind, but it was someone who obviously wanted me to remember that people do care.

I firmly believe that mankind is so instinctively, unconsciously involved with the survival and growth of the species that when an individual attempts to live selfishly, he will either fail or fall into despair.
—Joyce Carol Oates

*O*ne night I was working late at the office with a deadline staring me in the face. I slipped out to a local restaurant for a quick bowl of soup, which I ate sitting at the bar. There was only one other person there—a thin, middle-aged man with longish gray hair who seemed very sad. Politely, but with an edge of desperation, he was trying to get a conversation going with the bartender. She wasn't all that busy, but she seemed preoccupied and answered his questions very curtly.

I was torn between the desire to offer some comfort and the knowledge that I would

Waste no more time talking about great souls and how they should be. Become one yourself!
—Marcus Aurelius

already be up half the night meeting my deadline. I compromised. Next to my bowl of soup I left a five-dollar tip and a note saying, "Be nice to that man. He is very lonely."

I thought no more about it. A few months later I went to the home of a seamstress who had been recommended to me. When she opened the door I saw that it was the bartender. She recognized me immediately, smiled, and invited me in. There on the living room couch sat the man who had been at the bar. They both laughed at my surprise. She pointed to the mantlepiece and there, resting in a place of honor, was the note I had written to her.

For us, there is only the trying.
The rest is not our business.
—T. S. Eliot

*T*he woman bus driver for the morning commute downtown had a reputation for being crusty and unpleasant. One morning a very pretty teenage girl got on the bus. In a matter of moments everyone on the bus was gagging—the girl smelled terrible and appeared to be completely unaware of it. Every morning for a week the girl would get on the bus and riders would open windows, scurry to get off, and even make cruel comments.

One day our bus driver took control. As the girl was waiting to get off at her stop, the driver leaned over and spoke very softly to her. She said she knew she was doing the best she could and that she knew how it felt to be left out because she was different; then she gave the girl some specific hygiene suggestions. The next day she gave her a small bag full of assorted toiletries and even offered to buy her some new underwear when the girl told her she didn't have any. The bus driver really touched something in this youngster and all of us regular passengers saw empathy and kindness in our bus driver that we had never noticed before.

Now we all treat the young girl with much more kindness, and I called the transit authority to tell them how courteous, safe, and helpful our driver is. If by any chance she has anything amiss in her personnel file, I wanted to at least balance that and give her a break, just as she went out of her way to give that girl a break.

I am larger, better than I thought.
I did not know I held so much goodness.
—Walt Whitman

I was riding home from work on a crowded bus one day and found myself sitting next to an eight-year-old boy. He began singing quietly to himself, and as I listened I realized that he was singing his own song: "Today is my birthday, no one knows that it's my birthday, today is my birthday." I looked at him and said, "Is this really your birthday?" He got a big smile on his face and said yes. Then he started to cry and told me that he lived with his mother but that she wouldn't even remember it was his birthday because she was on drugs.

It is our special duty,
that if anyone needs our help,
we should give him such help to the utmost of our power.
—Cicero

He told me that last year his teacher had given him a pair of socks for his birthday and that was the best present he ever had. I wanted to give him something, but when I looked into my purse all I had was $6.25 and I needed $1.25 for my next bus. So I gave him the five-dollar bill and said, "I want you to go buy yourself something just for your birthday." He looked at me and thanked me, saying he would never forget this birthday. As he was getting off at his stop, he turned back and smiled at me and said, "I'm going to go buy myself some socks."

What we give to the poor . . .
is what we carry with us when we die.
—Peter Marin

My son Tom was killed in the Vietnam War. When we received the news, my wife and the two children still at home had a very difficult time dealing with it. Throughout the waiting for his body to be returned home, the arrangements for burial, and the transition back into a semblance of normal life, I was the pillar of strength and stability. I thought I was just doing what I had been trained to do—stay strong and calm—but in reality I was scared to death to show any emotion at all out of fear that I would collapse into an emotional morass from which I could never recover.

The key word for our time is practice. We have all the light we need, we just have to put it into practice.
—*Peace Pilgrim*

As time went by I grew increasingly depressed and distant, even from my own family. I hardly knew what was happening. Life seemed very gray and joyless. Then one day about four months after the funeral, I received a call from a young man named Brad who had been a very close friend of my son. He asked if he could come over and I of course agreed, not really understanding what he wanted to talk about. When he arrived we spoke awhile about things Tom had liked to do and he told me some special memories from his relationship with Tom. Then he walked over, hugged me, and with tears streaming down his face said, "I just miss him so much."

I will not keep silence, but will recompense.
—Isaiah lxv.6

Something inside me gave way and I broke down sobbing in this young man's arms. I cried and cried uncontrollably until it felt like my insides would spill out all over the floor. The two of us spent most of the afternoon in my study crying, talking, laughing, being embarrassed, crying some more, being embarrassed by being embarrassed, and finally, in a beautifully drained and painful state, just remembering how much we loved Tom and how much it hurt to have him gone.

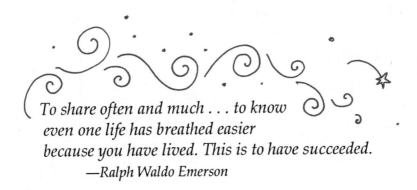

*To share often and much . . . to know
even one life has breathed easier
because you have lived. This is to have succeeded.*
    —*Ralph Waldo Emerson*

One night around midnight in my third year of high school I was driving through a very rich neighborhood when I spotted a small boy walking along the road. He seemed so out of place that I pulled over to see if he needed any help. When I opened my door I could see that he was about eight years old and was crying. I asked him where he was going and if he needed a ride home, but he wouldn't answer me. Finally I just said, "Here, get in the car and we'll go get some ice cream or something." He quite willingly got in, but then wouldn't answer anything more than yes or no.

Before starting the car, I got a twenty-dollar bill out of my purse and told him to hold it until we found an ice cream store. Then as we were searching, I kept asking where he lived and offering to take him home. Finally he said, "No, please, they're mean to me. I ran away."

I asked him if he lived with both his parents, and he told me that he lived with his father and stepmother. He said he wanted to be with his mother, but she lived in Texas.

We drove around for about an hour, never finding an open ice cream store, and he still refused to be taken home. Finally he told me where his best friend lived, so I took him there and gave him my phone number. On the way back to the car I remembered the twenty-dollar bill I had given him and assumed he

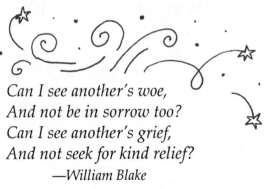

Can I see another's woe,
And not be in sorrow too?
Can I see another's grief,
And not seek for kind relief?
        —William Blake

still had it. When I got in the car the money was lying on the passenger seat. I remember smiling, hoping he would be okay and thinking that he had probably just had a fight with his father.

A week later I got a call from his friend's parents, telling me that they had found iron burns across his back and other cuts and bruises. He ended up being sent to his mother in Texas after a big court battle. It made me feel so blessed to have been able to play a part in helping him escape from the brutal world he had been living in.

If we make our goal to live a life of compassion and unconditional love, then the world will indeed become a garden where all kinds of flowers can bloom and grow.
—Elisabeth Kübler-Ross

The contractions came on quickly. I got to the hospital without incident, only to find that my doctor was not around. This was my third child and the labor was rapid and intense. For three hours the contractions built and still my obstetrician had not shown up. It was pretty obvious that this child wasn't going to wait. One of the interns (I never saw her) stood behind me and began stroking my cheek. Such a simple act.

That was thirty-one years ago and the memory has stayed with me ever since. There in the midst of the daily business of a hospital, some wonderful person reached out to a scared woman in pain, stroked her cheek, and gave a gift of human comfort that has lasted for so many years.

How rarely we weigh our neighbor in the same balance in which we weigh ourselves.
—*Thomas à Kempis*

I did not go through my teenage years gracefully. I was overweight and pear-shaped with glasses, braces, and acne. My self-consciousness was aggravated by my little sister who was ten years younger than me and so pretty with her apple cheeks and long auburn ringlets that people would stop us on the street just to admire her. One day one of my mother's friends, whom I adored because she was so sophisticated and stylish and because she always treated me as a person rather than as a child, complimented me on my eyebrows. She told me that they were so dark and beautifully shaped that they made me look very exotic. Forty years later that single compliment—given so freely and sincerely to a child who did not feel at all attractive or exotic—still fills my heart with gratitude.

*T*o many people civil servants and lawyers rank at the bottom of the list of those from whom you would expect unsolicited acts of kindness. Jerry Curtis knows better. Curtis, a fifty-year-old assistant attorney general with the Department of Justice, had been battling serious stomach problems and cancer of the lymph system. He was operated on and then began a lengthy regimen of chemotherapy. The treatment left him weak and vulnerable. He tried to go back to work but was unable. Within a couple months all his sick leave had been depleted and he was forced to get by on what savings he had.

One day Jerry found a check from his employer in his mailbox. It turned out that fellow Department of Justice employees from all over the state had donated four months of their collective sick leave and vacation pay to ensure that Jerry could focus on recovering his health without having to worry about how he was going to pay his bills.

"These people are so decent," said Jerry. "People I did not even know donated their time. It is just overwhelming; it's very difficult to describe how I feel. It's one of the strongest expressions of decency I've ever known people to make, and I don't even know who did it; I can't even give it back to them if I don't use it all. But if someone else needs it, you know I'm going to be the first one to donate it."

Kindness is charity minus money.
—Max Gralnick

I don't know what it was about the oddly mismatched group that caught my attention. It was not big enough to be a demonstration, and the makeup of the group—multiracial and spanning every generation—precluded most of the standard social groupings. There were less than thirty of them walking together through one of the less desirable neighborhoods in town, one that had seen more than its share of violence in the last few years. As I slowly drove by, they stopped and gathered around a large sidewalk with shade trees.

There is an imperative which commands a certain conduct immediately, without having as its condition any other purpose to be attained by it. This imperative is Categorical . . . This imperative may be called that of Morality.
— *Immanuel Kant*

For some reason I stopped, got out of my car, and walked over to see what was going on. As I approached I could hear a very old woman reminiscing about a young man. She had known him as he was growing up in the neighborhood, not well, but enough to have talked with him quite a few times over the years, and enough to bring tears to her eyes now.

It turned out this odd collection of people were all from the neighborhood and were on a march of remembrance—walking through the streets, stopping at the place where someone had died, to re-member and leave a wreath, some flowers, and some-times a note or small sign. Most of the deaths were of young men, lives wasted by too easy access to guns and drugs and too little under-

Be the change you want to see in the world.
—*Gandhi*

standing of the sacredness of human life. Wreaths and crosses hung from trees, marking spots where moments of stupidity ended in tragedy.

It was a tearful procession, but it was also a march of hope. Memorializing those who died, removing them from the world of statistics, and remembering them for a moment as people—a part of our community—was an act of healing and a step toward a neighborhood at peace.

The perfume of sandalwood,
the scent of rosebay and jasmine,
travel only as far as the wind.
But the fragrance of goodness travels with us
through all the worlds. Like garlands woven from a heap
of flowers, fashion your life
as a garland of beautiful deeds.
—the Buddha

The tired-looking man in well-worn clothes stood at the intersection wearing a large sign that read, "HAVE FAMILY, WILL WORK FOR FOOD." I had passed him many times as I made my way around town, yet somehow I never got around to offering help to this fellow traveler as I went about my busy week.

One day as I was going past the same intersection, I saw him once again steadfastly standing there. The traffic had stopped for a red light, and in the lane to my left a woman quickly got out of her car with two full bags of groceries which she promptly

Oh I am a cat that likes to
Gallop about doing good.
—*Stevie Smith*

handed to the man. They exchanged a few words before the light changed, and she jumped back in her car and drove away. The man's face lit up, his weariness lifted by this unknown woman's kindness. Carefully hugging the groceries, he slowly walked away from the crossroad; his radiant smile said it all.

In a fraction of a moment's time his life had been changed—and hers, and mine, and everyone else who sat in their cars and witnessed the exchange. The traffic still flowed, everything was the same, yet it was so very different.

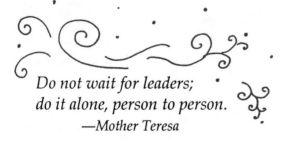

Do not wait for leaders;
do it alone, person to person.
—Mother Teresa

*A*nyone who has ever played basketball knows that playing with no net really takes some of the fun out of it. You just don't get that great *whoosh* feel when the ball drops straight through a naked hoop. But this didn't deter some teenage boys in our neighborhood who were regularly in their driveway, tossing the ball through an empty hoop. One day a neighbor they didn't know stopped in front of their house, rolled down the window, handed them a basketball net, called out "Merry Christmas," and drove off. The boys just stood there staring at the net in their hands—but not for long! Every now and then they interrupt their game to wave at their new friend as he drives by and then—*whoosh*—nothing but net.

He does well who serves the common good rather than his own will.
—*Thomas à Kempis*

I was a teenage runaway. I was trying to get off the streets, where I'd been hiding from the pimps and others who tried to take advantage of my situation, and ended up hitchhiking to a job interview. After my interview I planned to stop by the plasma center to get money from donated blood so I could eat. A man stopped to pick me up and, despite my strong negative gut reaction, I didn't want to miss my interview so I got in the car.

We drove down the highway a few miles, and he asked me a lot of questions. He wanted to

The center of human nature is rooted in ten thousand ordinary acts of kindness that define our days.
—Stephen Jay Gould

know how much I got paid for donating blood, and I told him it was $9. Then he said I could either be raped or he'd give me $9 to have sex with him. I was so scared I just grabbed the door, opened it, and jumped out. It surprised him so much that he slowed down enough for me to avoid getting seriously hurt. I was, however, scared and badly shaken. I started walking down the highway feeling lucky to have escaped but wondering when I'd ever feel like a human being again.

I remember your saying that you had notions of a good Genius presiding over you. I have of late had the same thought—for things which [I] do half at random are afterwards confirmed by my judgement in a dozen features of propriety.
—John Keats

Not a minute later a van pulled over and a man with his young daughter asked me if I needed a ride. He'd seen me falling out of the car and he asked what had happened. After I told him, he said how sorry he was and congratulated me on my escape. After a few miles he said he had a short stop to make; he came back with three huge, bright red apples, one for each of us. We ate as he drove me right to my interview. He wished me luck and I never saw him again.

I got the job! That was thirteen years ago, and I'm still with the company and doing better than I ever imagined possible. Right when things looked as bad as they had ever looked, that kind stranger gave me the lift I needed.

Good will is the best charity.
—*Yiddish proverb*

*A*ll of my adult life has been spent working with the very poor and being filled over and over by those whom I have chosen to serve. I often do outreach among the homeless living in our local transit hub, trying to get as many as possible into shelters. Many of these people are afraid to go to shelters for fear of losing their few belongings, but do not hesitate to sleep in the station because they look out for each other. When someone new arrives, the "regulars" are always

I think it pisses God off if you walk by the color purple in a field somewhere and don't notice it.
—*Alice Walker*

available to assist him or her. Underwear and socks are like solid gold to the homeless, yet I cannot begin to tell you how many times I have seen someone give their spare pair to someone who had none.

I have never ceased being awed by their great ability to serve. One day during the evening rush hour a woman who was dressed in a very business-like manner, obviously rushing home from work, tripped and fell in a very public area. Other well-dressed people continued on their way, even though it meant passing by her fallen body. But all the homeless folks in the area rushed to her assistance, helped her up, offered to make a phone call and get her medical assistance if she needed it. I could fill volumes with the stories I have been privileged to encounter. They give from their nothingness and with great freedom.

A few years ago my three-year-old son had a nasty fall and ended up at the local hospital. It turned out that the fall was the least of our worries. The doctors found a tumor the size of a softball in his left lung. We were all scared to death, and the doctors were none too optimistic. Throughout this traumatic development a male nurse showed great compassion toward my son.

Surgery was ordered immediately for the next day, and my son had to go through a tough procedure to get him ready. To my distress the wonder-

Kindness is the golden chain
by which society is bound together.
—Goethe

ful nurse was just about to sign off for the day, and the nurse replacing him was one who hated her job; I casually mentioned to the man that I wished he was going to be on duty instead.

A little while later he reappeared and stayed with us, helping out even though he was off duty. He even arranged to change his shift the next day so that when my son came out of surgery he would be there to soothe his fears. I will never forget what he did, and today when I look at my son, who is better than anyone thought possible, I truly believe that the sincere caring of this nurse was instrumental in his being able to keep trying.

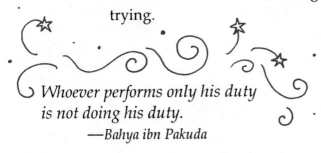

Whoever performs only his duty is not doing his duty.
—Bahya ibn Pakuda

*W*hen I was twelve years old I ended up in a Shriner's hospital in a full body cast, lying flat on my back for six months. I was surrounded by wonderful people doing everything they could to help me. One particular Sunday we had a scheduled picnic outdoors, and all the kids were brought outside for hamburgers, hot dogs, and a magic show.

My bed was wheeled outside, but by time the magic show was about to start I found

Tell them, that, to ease them of their griefs,
Their fear of hostile strokes, their aches, losses,
Their pangs of love, with other incident throes
That nature's fragile vessel doth sustain
In life's uncertain voyage, I will some kindness do them.
—Shakespeare

myself staring right into the sun, forcing me to close my eyes and cover them with my hands. Suddenly the sun seemed to disappear, and I opened my eyes to find a Shriner purposefully standing in a position that completely blocked the sun and still allowed me to see the stage. He stood there for the entire hour of the show—directly in line with the sun and shading his eyes with his hand.

This happened many years ago, but I have never forgotten what that man did to allow a little girl to witness the magic of magic and the magic of kindness.

It is impossible to pretend that you are not heir to, and therefore, however inadequately or unwillingly, responsible to, and for, the time and place that give you life.
—*James Baldwin*

*T*wo years ago a sixty-eight-year-old woman was the victim of a burglary. She lived simply on a fixed income, and the only item of value—her television—was stolen. After saving for nearly a year she bought a new one. Then, returning home one afternoon from a visit with her sister, she found a police officer waiting for her. Her home had been burglarized again, and again her television had been taken; this left her scared, shaken, and without access to what was a regular part of her day.

This time the story turned out differently. After hearing her plight, the officer in charge of the investigation took up a collection at the police station and negotiated a deal with a local electronics store that resulted in a brand-new television arriving in time for her sixty-ninth birthday.

When I was ten years old I went to summer camp for the first time. That school year had been very difficult for me: for reasons I never understood, I had become the girl everyone loved to tease. I was isolated, called names, and even beat up as I walked home from school. But I was excited about summer camp and vowed to make everyone there like me.

Well, it happened again. Three days at camp and a couple of girls snuck into my suitcase while I was in the shower and threw my underwear all over the cabin. The counselors did their best to console me but I was hysterical and couldn't understand why everyone hated me.

What do we live for, if it is not to make life less difficult for each other?
—*George Eliot*

A couple of nights later at one of our campfire sing-alongs, I was sitting alone. I enjoyed singing and we were doing this beautiful John Denver song that really comforted me. I sat there singing quietly to myself when an older camper from California came over and asked if she could sit by me. It made me feel so special. Here was this older girl who wanted to sit by me!

They were handing out awards that night and I was hoping for the "Songbird" award that

You have not lived a perfect day,
even though you have earned your
money, unless you have done something
for someone who will never be able to repay you.
—*Ruth Smeltzer*

went to the best singer at camp. When it went to another girl who happened to sing much louder than I, I was devastated. Then my new friend sitting beside me announced to everyone that "Angela has a beautiful voice too!" It felt so good to have someone give me a compliment in front of everyone. She also told me that she wanted to sit next to me because she loved to hear me singing and thought I was the nicest girl at camp.

I don't remember her name and I never saw her again after that summer but I know I never thanked her properly for the wonderful kindness she showed to me.

Then cherish pity, lest
you drive an angel from your door.
—*William Blake*

I used to suffer from vertigo. My fear of heights was not something I ever anticipated; it would just come over me. I never gave it any thought until suddenly I found myself reeling with dizziness or paralyzed and unable to move. One day I was walking to an appointment when I came to an overpass. It wasn't even that high, but I could not cross it. I stood there feeling foolish and helpless. I wanted to keep the appointment but there I was, frozen, unable to proceed.

A woman crossing from the opposite direction with her small son noticed me standing there is obvious distress and came over to me. "Are you all right?" she asked. "Oh, I feel so foolish," I said, "but I have a fear of heights and I can't cross this bridge." "Would it help if I crossed with you?" she asked. Taking my arm, she and her son walked back across the bridge with me. That happened twenty years ago, but I'll always remember that woman.

I am a senior in high school and work at an athletic-shoe store. One day a woman and her six-year-old son came in to buy school shoes. They found a pair he liked and came to the register to pay for them. As she was unfolding her checkbook I noticed they were temporary checks and I had to tell her that store policy would not let me accept her check.

Her son had been prancing around the store, testing out his new shoes and showing them to everyone; when she told him he had to take them off, tears started to well up in his eyes. It just broke

A soul occupied with
great ideas best performs small duties.
—Harriet Martineau

my heart. I stopped him before he could untie them, and pulled out my checkbook and wrote a check for the shoes. His mother could not believe what I was doing. She wrote a temporary check out to me and gave me her address and telephone number so I would know that I could trust her.

As she walked out of the store she told me she would never forget me. It was not until later that I noticed she had made out the check for ten dollars more than the shoes cost. And at the bottom of the check on the memo line she had written: "For the nice woman at the shoe store."

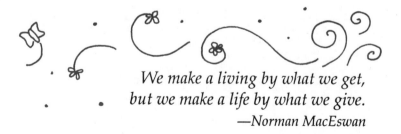

We make a living by what we get,
but we make a life by what we give.
—*Norman MacEswan*

I drive a taxicab in San Diego and have seen thousands of acts of kindness. One of the most wonderful came when the stepfather of our dispatcher died, and the dispatcher could not afford the money to fly back to New Jersey for the funeral. All day long pledges of money kept coming in over the radio. It was just like a private telethon. Cab drivers and even passengers who heard what was happening over the radio started emptying their pockets. We raised the plane fare in no time.

*Help me to fling my life
like a flaming firebrand into the
gathering darkness of the world.*
—Albert Schweitzer

The simplest acts of kindness can have such a powerful impact. Some years ago I was trying to work my way through college selling children's books door to door in Florida. One particularly blistering day nothing seemed to go right. I had knocked on every door for blocks without a single answer; I was hot, tired, and hungry, and felt like a total failure. I wanted nothing more than to quit my job and run home to the Midwest. I wasn't even thinking about selling books—I just wanted a glass of water and place to rest for a few minutes.

I looked down the street at a small white house and was drawn toward it. I had barely knocked on the

The end result of wisdom is . . . good deeds.
—*Babylonian Talmud*

door when an older woman opened it and immediately asked me in. She gave me a drink and invited me to share a meal with her and her husband. It was obvious that they did not have much money.

During the two hours I was there, the woman and her husband shared stories of the hardships and experiences in their lives and told me that it was very important to always love and care deeply about others—even strangers. As I left, the man gave me money and said he just wanted to help me out and that he had no need for my books. As I walked back down the street I broke into tears and sobbed for blocks. These people who at first seemed to have so little

had given me more than I could ever have asked for.

I am an immigrant from the old Soviet Union. I brought with me many dreams and misconceptions and, I am sad to admit, some prejudices. One day after I had been here for only a very short while I had spent what seemed at the time to be a very large sum of money on a "Fast Pass" bus ticket to make sure I could always get to school and around town. I had just bought it and when I returned home it was gone. I don't know how or where I had lost it; and even though I had put my name and address on it, I knew that anyone else could use it very easily. I had to face the fact that it was gone. I felt very depressed.

Then the doorbell rang. Standing there was a black woman with my Fast Pass in her hand. She told me she had found it on the sidewalk a few blocks away and handed it to me. At that moment everything changed. I will never again generalize about people because of their color and I will never forget that woman.

*L*ast year I had occasion to get acquainted with a homeless man who lived at the top of a freeway offramp in Los Angeles. Every day on my way to work as I sat waiting for the light to change I would talk to Ed about life, homelessness, hopefulness, and the weather—the weather being of vital importance to Ed. We became close, always asking about each other's family—mine in L.A., his on the East Coast. He rarely asked me for money, and I usually tried to bring him some food. Once when he had dental problems I brought him bananas, dried soup, and aspirin. Ed had many other "regulars" who tried to help out.

When I decided to leave L.A. for a

Each day the first day:
Each day a life.
—Dag Hammarskjöld

job in Florida, I had one final detail to attend to—my car. It was an ugly 1972 Dodge Dart, but it ran great. I had put a lot of money into it but the most I could get out of it was $90 from a wrecking yard. I wanted it to go to someone who could and would make use of it, and Ed was the logical choice. He had dreams and plans; he wanted to return to trade school—he had had to drop out earlier when his books were stolen, then the bus schedules changed and they no longer went by the trade school.

The week before I left I made Ed the offer of the car or the money from the junkyard, whichever he wanted. With enthusiasm he accepted the car, going on and on about it being his house

Dig within.
Within is the wellspring of Good;
and it is always ready to bubble up, if you just dig.
—*Marcus Aurelius*

and the answer to his problems. We took care of the paperwork, I paid for his license renewal, and then delivered the car with cans of oil, air and oil filters, and a trunk (he calls it his garage) full of paper plates, paper towels, canned food, clothes and—an L.A. essential—an earthquake kit.

As we stood next to the car on a Saturday morning, Ed said he had worked out a deal with a local parking-lot owner; he would sweep the lot every day in exchange for a covered place to park his "house." He also told me that he had just been offered a job as a dishwasher in a new upscale restaurant near his offramp. It turns out that another driver who regularly gave Ed money and food had bought the restaurant and asked him to work there at a really good wage. As we hugged good-bye, I said, "Ed, it looks like your ship has come in." He replied with tears in his eyes, "Hell, it's not only come in, I get to go on board."

I had been traveling in Asia for three months and was in Hong Kong to meet up with my boyfriend who was flying in for a week. Somehow his pending arrival had brought up all the homesickness that had stayed buried during the day-to-day difficulties and joys of traveling. I had boarded a bus that I thought was going to the airport, but the bus flew past the airport without stopping and I burst into tears. I was eager to meet my boyfriend's flight but instead I was on a bus to god knows where. I kept calling out "airport, airport," but the bus driver spoke no English.

A Chinese woman who spoke some

Love has nothing to do with what you are expecting to get—only what you are expecting to give.
—Katharine Hepburn

English told me to get off at the next stop which was in the middle of an expressway. The woman exited and headed off in the opposite direction, after indicating that I was to follow a second woman who was gesturing wildly and speaking Chinese. Then she too turned off in a different direction after aiming me down still another street. After a few steps I noticed an old man who had been there all along. Quietly and patiently, looking back every so often to make sure I didn't get lost, he guided me through the crowded and confusing streets of Kowloon to the airport. To this day I think gratefully of my shy and silent guide and of course his more vocal friends.

It's no use trying to be clever—
we are all clever here;
just try to be kind—a little kind.
—*Dr. F.J. Foakes Jackson*

*M*any years ago my husband and I relo-cated to California. As we were preparing to move, I was warned many times to "watch out for those long-haired, drug-crazed hippies." Shortly after our arrival our new neighbors took us to a hidden beach they had found near Half Moon Bay. It was a beautiful cove that was accessible only by going down a steep, sandy embankment. We had a wonderful day and built a great driftwood campfire; as the temperatures began to drop and the fog started rolling in, we decided to head home. My husband and our neighbors packed up the coolers and blankets and began the strenuous trek up the embankment. I followed, carrying my baby daughter while my cranky two- and four-year-olds struggled through the shifting sand.

We were soon left behind and within moments ground to a discouraging halt—the four of us close to tears. Suddenly up at the top of the hill two such "long-haired hippies" appeared. My heart stopped. I felt completely defenseless, alone—stuck partway up a steep embankment with three small children. The young man quickly took off his backpack, scurried down the hill, and to my horror grabbed my oldest son, hoisted him onto his shoulders, and climbed back to the top, where he handed him to the young girl accompanying him. He returned twice to pick up my other two children and ferry them to solid ground before returning one more time. He looked me straight in the eye and said, "Are you alright?"

I realized that he was more than ready to pick me up and carry me to the top of the hill as well! I laughed and assured him that relieved of my burden I could make it myself. I thanked him, and as it turned out, they were searching for a place to camp that evening. I hope our well-built campfire warmed them as much as their sweet assistance warmed me.

*M*y ten-year-old grand-daughter Anika is a big baseball fan. I have cable television and we have spent many a wonderful time together rooting hard for a Cubs victory. She also plays on a local girls' softball team and practices her batting in my backyard. My dog is the "catcher" and dutifully returns any errant pitches to the pitcher.

A couple of years ago we were

The world is in desperate need of human beings whose own level of growth is sufficient to enable them to learn to live and work with others cooperatively and lovingly, to care for others—not for what those others can do for you or for what they think of you, but rather in terms of what you can do for them.
—Elisabeth Kübler-Ross

shopping the baseball card collection at an antique show and Anika really wanted this Ryne Sandberg card—he is our favorite player and Anika even had a number 23 stitched onto her sweatshirt. After some discussion, however, we decided that $5 was just more than we could afford, so we handed the card back and continued to discuss the other cards. Out of nowhere a hand reached in with "the card" and a five-dollar bill, and the man turned to my granddaughter and said, "Happy next birthday!" He turned and was gone before we could even thank him.

Kindness is the better part of goodness.
—William Somerset Maugham

*S*ome years ago while driving home alone in my Volkswagen beetle the car suddenly lost power. I coasted to a stop on the shoulder, got out, and saw only cornfields for miles in every direction. After a while a car pulled over and a man got out and asked in a thick Irish brogue, "Would you be needin' help?" I quickly explained to him what had happened and he said, "I'll have a look, shall I?"

All hope of rescue died as he opened the hood to find no engine. I explained that the engine was in the back, and without missing a beat he shifted position and tinkered around for a few minutes

The fragrance of the rose lingers on the hand of the giver.
—*Anonymous*

and then popped his head up and said, "I've just what's needed." He returned to his car and, after rummaging around, returned with a roll of Scotch tape. I just stood there in disbelief as he dived back into the engine compartment to apply his magic remedy.

"Start 'er up." I complied, and the engine roared to life. He waved my thanks aside and followed me all the way back into town. When I finally got my car to a mechanic, it took them a full ten minutes to find what he had taped.

We aspire to . . . act with the eyes and heart of compassion. . . . We know the happiness of others in our own happiness. . . . We know that every word, every look, every action, and every smile can bring happiness to others.
—*Thich Nhat Hanh*

*W*hen I was eight years old my family moved. I was the new kid coming into a new school and was pretty nervous, but the transition turned out to be a wonderful one. On my first day my teacher turned me over to a classmate named Beth with instructions to introduce me around. Beth made me feel so welcome; she and I quickly became best friends.

She got me to try out for cheerleader with her and taught me how to do backward handsprings. For a few years we were inseparable.

Giving is so often thought of in terms of the things we give, but our greatest giving is of our time, and kindness, and even comfort for those who need it. We look on these gifts as unimportant—until we need them.
—Joyce Sequichie Hifler

Then one day we had a fight—the kind that seems so big and important to kids—and although we remained friends, the special bond was broken and gradually we drifted apart.

By the time I was a sophomore in high school, Beth and I moved in different circles. Then that year she was killed in an car accident. I was overwhelmed by the hurt, which was so much more difficult because I was left alone with my grief. Not being one of Beth's current friends, I was outside the circle of close friends mourning her death.

Always, Sir,
set a high value on spontaneous kindness.
—*Samuel Johnson*

Last year I graduated from high school, and Beth's mother came to see me. She brought me $50 from Beth's life savings as a graduation gift. She told me she wanted to give a little something of Beth to her closest friends. Then she had a party for all Beth's old friends to give us a chance to get back together and remember why we were friends in the first place.

Beth's mother's act of kindness changed me forever. Not only did she give me a part of Beth, but she gave me the comfort, acceptance, and understanding that I had not received two years earlier when Beth died. She taught me that you can never take love and friendship for granted and that they will always live in the hearts of those who experience their true meaning.

We must enhance the light, not fight the darkness.
—*Aharaon David Gordon*

In the mid-1980s, my husband and I were doing well financially. So we decided to take our Christmas money and do something to benefit someone who was in need. We knew a couple struggling with a failing business, three young children, and the possible loss of their home. We gave them money and told them that we did not want to be repaid but that when they got back on their feet, they could pass it on to someone else in need.

Just a few weeks later I met the recipient of our gift. She told me that part of our wish had already come true: They knew another family in even worse circumstances than they were in and had given half of our gift to them. What kindness! Our giving was from our surplus but their giving was from need.

When I was sixteen and learning how to drive, I motioned to a driver to go ahead of me, and he didn't acknowledge what I had done. Self-righteously I said, "I'll never do that again!" My father asked me to pull over, and said, "You're not kind to people because they'll thank you. You're kind to people because it's the right thing to do. You're kind to people because it helps the other person and because it helps you." That was fifteen years ago and I've tried to live my life from that perspective. I can still hear my father's gentle voice asking me, "Your attitude, action, comment—will it add to the sadness and hurt of the world? Or will it add to the love and the kindness which might heal us and make us whole? It's your choice."

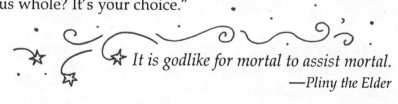

It is godlike for mortal to assist mortal.
—*Pliny the Elder*

I recently went through a painful yet relieving divorce after seventeen years of marriage. I needed a place to live with my two boys, and my sister and brother-in-law graciously suggested we move in with them. It was a wonderful thing for them to have done, but I soon realized that we needed to find a home of our own. But how could I afford it? A single mother with two children—rent, daycare, groceries, clothes, health insurance, car payments, etc., etc. . . . It seemed overwhelming but I knew in my heart that somehow it would work out.

One can never pay in gratitude;
one can only pay "in kind" somewhere else in life.
—Anne Morrow Lindbergh

I found a small house and proceeded to move in, not knowing how I was going to make ends meet. Two weeks later a dear friend stopped by my work. He had heard about my divorce and he and his wife wanted to help. He offered to pay the rent for me. I thought it was for one month, but every month I received a check from them for my rent.

It was such an unbelievably generous thing to do. He did not want me to repay him and asked only that if possible I return the favor to someone else in need someday. It turned out that when he was struggling in medical school someone had done this for him.

Give what you have,
To someone it may be better
Than you dare to think.
—*Henry Wadsworth Longfellow*

I was wandering aimlessly through the aisles of the automotive department of a Sears store in a big, impersonal East Coast city. I felt terribly alone, far from home, and so totally preoccupied with my own misery and loneliness that I don't think I really saw anything on the shelves. After awhile I became aware of a small child about three or four years old, walking and crying at my side. I don't know how long she had been keeping me company, but I sensed that somehow

What matters is that we recognize our smallness in the universe and see kindness as the only avenue toward a larger self.
—*Gloria Wade-Gayles*

she had gravitated toward me as someone who would help her. I knelt beside her and asked if she was lost; with tears streaming from her eyes, she just nodded. I held out my hand and told her not to worry, that we would find her parents. She put her hand in mine and I led her up to the counter, where two wonderful salesladies immediately enveloped her and promised to find her parents.

As I was leaving the store I heard the announcement over the paging system and had no doubt that she would soon be reunited with her parents. I also realized that all my own doom and gloom had disappeared. I thought to myself that just as that little girl had renewed my spirit, perhaps the small acts of strangers willing to help would allow this child to grow up with a little less fear and a more compassionate outlook on the world.

*S*ome years ago my daughter and I were living in Germany. We got word that some of her stateside high-school friends were coming on a "French trip" to Paris and the Loire Valley. We arranged to meet them in Paris, and after an exciting eight-hour train ride, we hooked up and had a fantastic time.

On the final day of their visit we ended up on a tour bus, dropping them all off at the airport with many tears and hugs, filled with the joy of the time we had spent together. My daughter and I, however, still had to get to the train station all the way across Paris to catch our train. We had originally arranged with the tour bus driver to drop us off at the first subway station, but everything that day seemed to take twice as long as we thought it would; we started worrying about getting to the station on time, particularly trying to struggle our way through the Paris Metro with our baggage, which was now overloaded with treasures.

If we missed the train, we would miss all our connections and not make it home in time for work and school the next day. Our bus driver—Ahmed—spoke very little English, but he must have seen that we were worried, because we sailed right past the Metro station and he drove us through the unbelievable mess of Parisian rush-hour traffic, delivering us to the front entrance of the train station with plenty of time to spare. He wouldn't even accept the extra money we offered him, but just wished us a safe journey. It was such a heartwarming act of kindness in a city with a reputation for being so brusk and impersonal.

A man can do only what a man can do. But if he does that each day he can sleep at night and do it again the next day.
—*Albert Schweitzer*

One Saturday evening I received a long-distance phone call and learned that a very close, dear friend had died tragically. The unexpected news was quite a blow. I was in terrible pain and tried calling my three sisters, hoping to find one of them at home. On my first two calls I got no answer. On my last call, my sister's son answered and, still trembling, I explained my reason for calling. He said he would try to find his mother for me. The next thing I knew there was a knock at my door—it was my nephew. All I remember for the rest of that night was sitting on the couch in his arms, crying for what seemed like an eternity while he quietly held me and comforted me. I think often of what a brave and compassionate young man he was that night—he gave me much more than he will ever know.

Say little and do much.
—*Shammai*

*I*n 1972 I was living in Utah, and my sister and I took a drive down to the Great Salt Lake—miles away from anything. When we got back to the car in the evening we noticed a very flat tire. We were both in our early twenties and had no idea how to fix it. While we were standing there wondering what to do, a gang of eight to ten guys on motorcycles roared over the rise and pulled to a halt right in front of us. We were scared to death—after all, we had watched enough television to know that this was not a good situation.

The leader of the group got off his bike, followed by three other big, burly, rough-looking men. He looked straight at us and

Be kind—everyone you meet is fighting a hard battle.
—*John Watson*

said, "Gimme your keys." With a sinking feeling of hopelessness, my sister handed them over. The four men then proceeded to change our tire while we watched. Then the leader came back, handed us the keys, and said, "Now go home." They roared off into the sunset, and ever since that day I am very careful not to judge people by how they look.

I have never given very deep thought
to a philosophy of life though I have a few ideas
that I think are useful to me:
Do whatever comes your way to do as well as you can.
Think as little as possible about yourself.
Think as much as possible about other people.
  —*Eleanor Roosevelt*

*O*ne year when I was away at school I had gone to the Greyhound bus depot to catch a bus home for Christmas break. I looked all over for the right bus, but none of the buses lined up at the terminal had my destination on them. As I was standing there trying to figure out where my bus was, one pulled out and the driver changed the sign as he was leaving—to exactly where *I* wanted to go. I stood there watching my bus disappear down the highway; I must have been visibly upset because a woman came over, took my arm, led me to the street, hailed a taxicab, gave the driver a five-dollar bill, and told him to get me over to the ferry dock quickly, because the bus made a stop there before heading out onto the highway. She wished me a Merry Christmas and all I could do was smile.

I had just moved out of a recovery house after spending six months battling an addiction to alcohol and drugs. I was standing at a bus stop looking through the classifieds, hoping to find a job I was capable of doing. Without a high-school education and with my work experience limited to waitressing, the options seemed depressingly limited. At that point my self-esteem was stuck to the bottom of my shoes and it diminished with each ad I read.

I looked up from the paper to see an elderly man sitting in his car. He asked me if I wanted

When I was young,
I admired clever people. Now that I am old,
I admire kind people.
  —Abraham Heschel

a ride and I accepted—knowing what a foolish thing I was doing and even secretly hoping that he would put an end to it all for me. He asked me where I was going and what I was doing. I said I did not know. Then he simply asked me, "If you could do anything you wanted to do, what would it be?"

I blurted out that I would go back to school. I immediately felt stupid for saying it because I doubted I ever could. A few minutes later he pulled into the parking lot of the local community college, pointed out the admissions office, and told me I would find what I needed in there. Trembling and insecure, I filled out the registration papers.

As I write this, I have received my associate of arts degree and am planning to study toward a bachelor's in journalism and a master's in psychology. My life has turned around 360 degrees, and I owe a lot of that to a man whose name I don't even know.

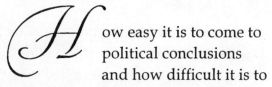

ow easy it is to come to political conclusions and how difficult it is to carry out some of those decisions in the world! Like many other border states, California has gone through its share of political pronouncements over the economic burden of illegal immigrants. The solutions have often been harsh, and, for a thirty-eight-year-old man named Enrique, threatened a death sentence.

Enrique slipped across the Mexican border three years ago with a dream common in this country: to work hard and make a better life for himself. He worked the fields of California and lived in the shadows of society, until he showed up at a

It's amazing how much people can get done if they do not worry about who gets the credit.
—Sandra Swinney

county hospital with a large tumor on the back of his head. Diagnosed with a treatable case of lymphoma, Enrique came up against a harsh reality: his cancer was completely curable, but without treatment he would be dead within six months and the state's "safety net" for medical treatment no longer pays to care for illegal immigrants.

Indeed, the hospital routinely turns away those too poor to pay, but Enrique's life-and-death plight caused many of the health-care professionals involved to pause and reconsider. Meetings were held, ethics debated. As his treating physician said: "Ethically, the situation is not at all unclear—this is a matter of life or death. If Enrique were a wealthier person or born in a different place, he'd be getting

To live, let live and help live.
—Ralph Waldo Emerson

treatment. The system has gotten so crazy that we can look at a young, healthy guy and say, 'Sorry.'"

But instead of saying sorry, a small group of health workers decided to do something about it. Doctors at the hospital donated their time to treat him, but the treatment itself—radiation, expensive drugs, and hospital stays—also cost a lot. So they approached a number of pharmaceutical companies and two offered to donate medication. Then they went public and donations began flowing in for the rest of the expenses.

Now Enrique will get his chance at life because enough people cared.

Even a poor man, a
recipient of charity, should give charity.
—*the Talmud*

I have always believed in guardian angels, but had no idea mine would be in the form of a gynecologist! I was devastated to learn at age nineteen that I had an incurable and painful ovarian disease. Many difficult decisions followed, and my experience with the medical community left me despairing and disheartened. I searched for ten years to find a physician who was not only know-ledgeable but compassionate, and I had nearly lost faith.

Then I noticed a story in the local paper about a new gynecologist who was establishing a practice in our small town. Hardened by my experience, I hesitated, but finally decided to go. To my amazement he said if it would help, I could stop by often just to chat—free of charge! The only suggestion I had ever received before for dealing with the nightmare was a new prescription for pain medication. Through his genuine concern this doctor managed to motivate a very depressed, overweight person in physical and emotional pain to return to life.

He kept careful track of my progress as I joined aerobics, lost weight, and became able to sleep through the night with less pain. When I needed a hysterectomy he held my hand during the anesthesia, sent flowers to my hospital room, and even reduced my bill when he found out my insurance would not cover it all.

Two years later my life feels worth living and I say a silent blessing of thanks each time I drive by his office.

When you become light and you radiate, there is no darkness. . . . If you burn yourself, you will radiate and will spread light. The job of the human being is to radiate through the finite self the infinite light.
—*Yogi Bhajan*

I was quietly working one day when I heard a very distressed voice coming from a nearby office. The walls were thin and I could not help but hear. A woman I did not know had been counting on borrowing money from a colleague but circumstances made it impossible for him to help her. I have no idea what possessed me, but without even asking what she needed it for I found myself going to the bank and withdrawing $1,000 to lend to a woman I did not even know.

Several months later after a series of life's ever-surprising turns, I found myself jobless, homeless, and, I thought, friendless. I also needed medical care in order to even begin looking for a new job. The woman to whom I had lent the money was not in a position to return it, but she ended up repaying me anyway—and then some. First, she had the medical training necessary to help me physically get back on my feet; then she had her son, who owned a small moving business, come collect my belongings, and arranged for her boyfriend to stay with her and deposited me in his apartment. I now had the three things a homeless person needs most: an address, a telephone, and a shower. As a bonus he had a lovely cat that went with the territory and gave me great comfort in that difficult time.

It wasn't too long before I was able to find work and move to a home of my own. That was thirteen years ago, and since then the woman and I have become life-long friends and eventually business partners. To her it was a miracle that anyone could give so much money to a stranger; to me it was a miracle that anyone could come up with such a basketful of solutions custom-made to fit my needs.

Independence? That's middle-class blasphemy. We are all dependent on one another, every soul of us on earth.
—*George Bernard Shaw*

As a person with meta-static breast cancer, some days are filled with anxiety and fear, but then some "random" thing will happen which gives me a lift. One time, for example, someone gave me an anonymous quote from "I Can Cope," a support organization for people living with cancer:

> *When we come to the edge*
> *Of all the light we have*
> *And we must take a step into*
> *The darkness of the unknown,*
> *We must believe one of two things:*
> *Either we will find something*
> *Firm to stand on*
> *Or we will be taught to fly.*

It reminded me that while I may frequently swoop and crash as I try to cope, my capacity for deeply meaningful exchanges even with strangers often allows me to fly naturally with no apparent instruments.

Sometimes I have something to give. One day, as I waited in my internist's office to see if he could provide me with a free sample of an antibiotic my oncologist had prescribed for an infection, the door opened and the doctor saw out a couple in their eighties. The woman was bent over in a wheelchair, the husband barely holding up on his feet behind her. He wheeled her to a couch that he sank into and I heard him say softly, "I am *so* tired."

"I know what you mean," I said, walking toward them, "when the fatigue is so great that everything goes into sheer self-maintenance and there's nothing left over for any meaning." I explained that I was a cancer patient in perpetual chemotherapy treatment and at times had that experience.

The secretary appeared at the window and I asked about the antibiotic. We talked while the doctor fetched the drug, and then I turned to go. To my astonishment, the elderly man looked transformed. His face had light and life in it. He smiled at me and said a couple of kindly sentences that I've now forgotten. My understanding and acknowledging his experiences had given him a moment of fresh energy.

Then there was the day in the cancer center when I sat across from a young man who was about to have blood drawn. He was of an age and thin in a way that suggested he might have AIDS. He sat with his eyes closed. I thought, his veins aren't what they once were and he's trying to help himself through this moment.

I felt a deep connection to this young man and I wanted to say, "I love you" but I couldn't quite do it in that congested space where our knees almost touched and nurses threaded their way through the miniscule openings between patients. So I sat quietly, willing my "I love you" to reach him. Then my voice began to speak.

"I really like your colors," I said, "—those rich purple pants and your maroon tie-dyed socks that sing with them."

A smile stretched his thin lips and brought light to his face. "My socks match my under-shirt," he said with a dash of impish pleasure.

"I see it peeking out beneath your shirt. It is a perfect match. And how the pants and tie-dye play together."

He opened his eyes and took me in. "And *I* like your turquoise. Oh, what a color!" We were living now in the fragile yet palpable world of our re-flected colors. Suddenly, I saw freshly the only other visible colors in this white medical room.

"You can't see it, but your colors are drawing out their twins in the picture above your head," I told him.

His eyes focused above my head. "And your turquoise," he said, "is an extension of the sea in the picture over you."

His procedure ended. Our trance was broken, but I believe we flew together in our momentary world of colors.

Constantly remind yourself, "I am a member of the whole body of conscious things." If you think of yourself as a mere "part," then love for humanity will not well up in your heart; you will look for some reward in every act of kindness and miss the boon which the act itself is offering. Then all your work will be seen as a mere duty and not as the very porthole connecting you with the Universe itself.
—*Marcus Aurelius*

Receiving
Random Acts of Kindness

The stories published in this book all came from letters we received. We edited, re-wrote, and polished, but a few resisted any editorial input.

*Y*our book *Random Acts of Kindness* has touched me deeply. As your book so beautifully demonstrates and, as your quote of the Dalai Lama says, kindness truly is a religion unto itself. What a beautiful moment it is when we can be in that space, no matter how brief. I am writing for two reasons: first, to relate a story of my own as you suggested at the end of the book; and second, to request permission to photocopy your book.

I am a prisoner at Bastrop Federal Prison. I have been in for seventeen years and only during the past two years have I allowed myself to open to the love which has been all around me my whole stay. I have had an assaultive and escape-filled past, and for the first fifteen years of my "vacation" I could have been accurately described as one of the coldest, most hardened men in the federal prison system.

Then one morning while passing our psychology department, Dr. Geraldine Nagy, a very attractive, petite, hundred-pound bundle of love and happiness stepped out of her office, turned, and almost ran into me (275 pounds). At first she was startled. We made eye contact, then a wonderful smile came across her face; she stuck out her hand and said, "Good morning, David." With, I'm sure, a dumbstruck look on my face, I shook her hand and said, "Good morning." I'm thinking: How the hell does she know my name? I've never gone near the shrink's office . . . . She starts to walk off, then turns back and says, "Do you ever smile?" I said, "Yeah, sometimes." She said, "Find somebody you feel comfortable with and try it today." She waved good-bye, smiled, and walked off.

Well, I did, and I know today that that moment of kindness changed my life. She and her husband, Dr. Allen Nagy, have over the past two years given and given and given of themselves and have handed my life back to its rightful owner—me.

They have established the only Holistic/Holographic Health Unit in the federal prison system which is just now beginning to receive the systemwide attention it deserves. It includes a "pro-values" unit—a one-year pilot program which will be evaluated for systemwide implementation. I and a core group of around a hundred other inmates, who have immersed ourselves in personal growth through their full-spectrum model from material to body to mind to soul to spirit, owe our lives to this tag team. They oper-ate from a position of unconditional love, understanding, and compassion.

Both Allen and Geraldine are doing groups based on your book. Our psych department doesn't have the funds to buy the needed twenty books, so I am writing to request permission to photocopy the whole book so everyone selected for the groups can have one. Dr. Allen Nagy was going to write to you, but as one of my three daily "acts," I offered to free up some of his time and write myself; besides, I wanted to tell you about my first contact with Geraldine and the open love I felt come from her.

I just graduated from high school, and this has been a very difficult and frustrating time in my life. I enjoy studying history and literature and someday want to study the philosophers as well, but I think way too much. Often I leave myself too much time alone for introspection and I begin to question everything. Lately my thoughts have tended more and more toward isolation and loneliness. I began feeling that every person I met was alien to me, as if their soul spoke a different language. Questions like what it really is to love were making me a very unhappy man; it felt as though I was no longer a member of the human race.

My mother gave me the book *Random Acts of Kindness* for a graduation present, and I broke down crying after only twenty-five pages. It made me realize that I really can feel love for another human being. I was just in hiding.

*T*hank you so much for your book *Random Acts of Kindness* and for your efforts to promote the kindness revolution. A few weeks ago this book was loaned to me by a member of my church choir of which I am the director. I immediately felt at home within its pages and have become an ambassador at large.

As I now must return the book to its original owner, I went searching for a copy which I could keep for myself and for a few extras to spread the wealth both personally and anonymously.

At the large book store I visited I was at a complete loss as to how to locate the book. When I approached the sales counter to ask for assistance a woman next to me in line upon hearing me ask for *Random Acts of Kindness* exclaimed "That's the name of it!" and after receiving directions to find the book, we went in search together. It seems that she had read and dearly loved the book, had given it to a friend, but could not recall the exact title and so had not been able to obtain another copy for herself.

We located the book, she purchased two copies, one to keep and one to give. I purchased five copies, one to keep and four to give. I don't expect this to be my last purchase!

We spent about ten minutes talking about the wonders that can be achieved by practicing random acts of kindness and the changes it has made in our lives. I asked if she had read Robert Fulghum's works ands she hadn't heard of them . . . once again we were on a search.

By the time we left the book store, I and this total stranger, we hugged and wished each other a beautiful life.

I have always considered myself a "kind and giving" person. As a matter of fact, I have a hand written "Commit a Random Act of Kindness" sign over my desk.

In two days I am going to the hospital to have "calcium clusters" removed for biopsy. I have been walking around in a "I'm a nice person—why is this happening to me?" funk of fear for weeks. Today while flying through the mall, I made my required trip to the book store—and there (with the Mother's Day books, of all things) was your book. As is my habit, I open a book at "random" to see if it speaks to me and what it has to say. I met the Russian grandmother in your book and took her home. My father came from Russia at the age of five. I took the book to my deck, put on some music, watched the geese swim in the pool, listened to my father speak through your pages, counted my blessings, vowed to be kinder and read away the fear—I had forgotten what was important—what was real—what matters. I had forgotten that the world does not revolve around me. That it still can turn out O.K.

So thank you, again. No matter what happens—I feel like a weight has lifted. And I'll be able to share happiness instead of fear.

Beyond the Toll Booth

When the phrase "Random Acts of Kindness" first started to surface in the media, the example most commonly used to explain it was that of paying the bridge toll for the car behind you. It is an apt metaphor—a simple act of kindness to ease the path of a total stranger.

When *Random Acts of Kindness* was first published, it had a number of lists of different "suggestions." We included them to spark the reader's own imagination of the many simple things that can be done to bring kindness alive. Since then, a handful of other books have appeared, adding more suggestions. This time, we have purposely not included any lists. Lists can be helpful, but they do not and cannot capture the heart of what it means to live with kindness.

Living each moment in the spirit of kindness is a deep and profound calling, one that resides at the very core of who we are. The challenge is to find ways to nurture that precious part of ourselves and to draw it more fully into the pattern of our daily lives.

The foundation of that process is to consciously practice the art of feeling and seeing yourself connected to others. It is easy to do at times and very difficult to maintain over time precisely because it is part and parcel of the paradox that lies at the heart of human existence—we are all uniquely ourselves, fascinatingly, wonderfully, and irritatingly different *and* we are all very much the same, tightly woven together in the vast web of humanity.

Connection implies at least two people open and willing, the giver and the receiver. Not surprisingly, one of the more important pieces of the process that we have found repeated by many of those who wrote to us is receptivity—being truly open to seeing people as they are rather than as we want or fear them to be, and therefore what is available to be received.

While being in a truly receptive state is often difficult—particularly in the face of upset or anger—the benefits are rich and rewarding. Not only can we see and feel our way past the surface turmoil, but we open ourselves to experience the incredible flood of beauty and caring that surrounds us on a daily basis.

The recognition of this connection to all of life is at the heart of random acts of kindness. Listen in to some of the profound "random acts" readers have told us about. They go way beyond toll booths:

"Walking across the park on my way to the bus stop one day, my feet danced through a hop-scotch pattern drawn in chalk on the pathway. Surprised at myself I looked up into the face of a small girl beaming the most beautiful radiant smile at me. It seems such a small thing but it felt like I had been touched by a magic wand."

"Listening to the second movement of Rachmaninoff's "Second Piano Concerto in C# Minor" for the first time at age thirteen, I knew that there was room in the world for all the feelings I was experiencing. No one else in my world could relate to those feelings, but Rachmaninoff helped me grow big enough to contain them all and still have room left over for sanity."

"The first time I saw a sculpture by Rodin, I couldn't keep my hands off it. I kept needing to touch the grace, touch the beauty. Until that moment I didn't know my hands could see."

"I grew up on a small boring farm and in the evenings I'd listen to late night disc jockeys playing rock and roll love songs. I'd huddle under my blankets listening and learned all about what I needed to know but could not find answers to anyplace else."

"My back was up against a tree—a tree I had sat with many times before—when suddenly a warm sensation went through my entire body. I felt truly embraced. Looking up at the magnificent canopy spreading out over my head, I saw for the first time that I was within the embrace of the strong vibrant beauty of the tree and had been each time I stopped there to rest."

Music, literature, a work of art, a stunning sunset, the sound of the wind in the trees, wildflowers growing out a crack in the sidewalk, children laughing, a smile on the street—we are surrounded in each moment by things that can reach down into our soul and make our hearts sing. All that holds us back is our own wariness and distraction.

Opening to becoming more receptive, learning how to feel connected with others more deeply, these are the cornerstones from which the inexhaustible wellspring of kindness will flow. For most of us the feeling comes most often and most easily with loved ones. When it happens, acknowledge it, cherish it, hold on to it as long as you can, and then try to figure out what brought that feeling into being, so you can expand the circle of connection with others without having to first be presented with a stranger's stark need.

We all need to find ways to incorporate kindness into our daily life; think expansively—the power of kindness is extraordinary. Just a "random" sampling:

• In the San Francisco Bay area, 1750 people come together to cook and deliver 2000 hot meals daily for those suffering with AIDS;

• In Indianapolis a man set up a program to recycle unused and broken bicycles to provide a way for kids to actually build themselves a bike they otherwise couldn't afford;

•Every year around the country, a program called Christmas in April organizes an army of volunteers to do major and minor repairs for those who can't do them themselves;

•In every city, church and community, groups feed the hungry every single day of the year.

Resolve to be an ambassador of kindness. Get together with friends and plot strategies for expanding your own personal sphere of influence, join with others in your community and participate in ways that feel meaningful to you in the programs and organizations that already exist to serve those in need. The needs are great, and the rewards even greater.

Random Acts of Kindness Day
is February 17, 1995

Conari Press is interested in promoting the cause of kindness wherever and however we can. To that end, we are sponsoring National Random Acts of Kindness Day on February 17, 1995 as part of National Random Acts of Kindness week recently proclaimed by the U.S. Congress.

Write us for your free packet on how you and your community, business, church, neighborhood or family group can participate:

Random Acts of Kindness Day
1144 65th St. Suite B.
Emeryville, CA 94608
(800) 685-9595
FAX: (510) 654-7259
e-mail: RAKDAY@aol.com

The Random Acts of Kindness Fund

We at Conari Press have made a commitment to donate 10% of the net proceeds from the sales of *Random Acts of Kindness, Kids' Random Acts of Kindness,* and *More Random Acts of Kindness* to a Random Acts of Kindness fund. Part of that fund will go toward promoting National Random Acts of Kindness Day, including giving books away to children and adults who normally can't afford them.

In compiling the three books, we were struck by how often random acts of kindness involved homeless people; perhaps they are the group in our society that is most visibly in need. Recognizing this, the greater portion of the fund will be given to VOLUNTEERS OF AMERICA, a national organization which helps relieve homelessness, and provides programs to assist

the elderly, families in crisis, abused children, the dis-
abled, as well as many others.

We thank you for your support of
our books and this ideal, and want you to be aware that
your purchase will continue the ripple of kindness. We
can all make change happen.

Free Button

Write to us also if you would like a
free button encouraging kindness. Please enclose a self-
addressed, stamped envelope.